Mannheim Steamroller

Christmas
Extraordinaire

PRAISE FOR *DEVELOPING EMPLOYEES WHO LOVE TO LEARN*

"*Developing Employees Who Love to Learn* has caused me to reconsider our approach to training . . . from the *learner's* perspective. Read Parts 1 and 2, then utilize Part 3, a compendium of ideas from which to select employee learning options for the employees in your organization."

> Larry Hoyt, Associate, Education & Development,
> GROWMARK, Inc.

"*Developing Employees Who Love to Learn* is an excellent resource for those who love to facilitate learning. Filled with sage practical advice, business examples, and a compendium of individual and team learning strategies, those who would create organizations that love to learn will find many excellent ideas in these pages."

> Karen E. Watkins, Professor, The University of Georgia, and
> coauthor of *Sculpting the Learning Organization*

"*Developing Employees Who Love to Learn* is a timely and constructive aid to frontline managers, human resource professionals, and others interested in continuous learning and improvement. Throughout the book there are exercises and checklists that provide structure to readers as they work on implementing learning within their organization."

> G. Wayne West, former Manager of Workforce Development,
> State of Ohio

Developing

Employees

Who Love

to Learn

Developing

Tools, Strategies,

Employees

and Programs

Who Love

for Promoting

to Learn

Learning at Work

LINDA HONOLD

DAVIES-BLACK PUBLISHING
Palo Alto, California

Published by Davies-Black Publishing, an imprint of Consulting Psychologists Press, Inc., 3803 East Bayshore Road, Palo Alto, CA 94303; 800-624-1765.

Special discounts on bulk quantities of Davies-Black books are available to corporations, professional associations, and other organizations. For details, contact the Director of Book Sales at Davies-Black Publishing, an imprint of Consulting Psychologists Press, Inc., 3803 East Bayshore Road, Palo Alto, CA 94303; 650-691-9123; fax 650-623-9271.

Visit the Davies-Black Publishing web site at www.daviesblack.com.

04 03 02 01 00   10 9 8 7 6 5 4 3 2 1
Printed in the United States of America

Library of Congress Cataloging-in-Publication Data
Honold, Linda
   Developing employees who love to learn : tools, strategies, and programs for promoting learning at work / Linda Honold.
         p. cm.
   Includes bibliographical references and index.
   ISBN 0-89106-150-9
   1. Employees—Training of. I. Title

   HF5549.5.T7 H616 2001
   658.3'124—dc21

                                                                00-031785
FIRST EDITION
First printing 2000

*To my husband, Reynolds, for his enduring love,
patience, and support*

Contents

Learning Tools

Foreword

Ralph Stayer

In recent years we have witnessed a dramatic explosion of how-to books proposing new methodologies, paradigms, and concepts for transforming the workplace. As managers take stock of what is required to be successful in today's work environment they look to the latest literature to help them rethink traditional "labor-management" behaviors—particularly those concerning how information is shared and applied. Unfortunately, most of what has been available misses the mark.

In my book *Flight of the Buffalo: Soaring to Excellence, Learning to Let Employees Lead,* I describe the lessons our company, Johnsonville Sausage, learned in the course of changing from a traditionally structured organization to one in which individuals know the common goal, take turns leading, and adjust their roles to the tasks at hand. My vision involved the creation of an organization where every person is committed to realizing the full use of his or her talents. We've discovered that true learning encourages us to question our own actions and behaviors in ways that increase our understanding of how we perform, work, and live. Such learning takes us out of the known and into the unknown and allows us to create effective change in our lives and our organizations in unpredictable ways. Perhaps the single most important ingredient in our successful transformation has been embedding the desire to learn.

Finding the right systems to encourage that vision and desire to learn remains a challenge for many organizations. Clearly transformation cannot be accomplished in a two-week training or relegated to a particular place and time. It cannot be dictated from the top down. Rather, it must grow from day-to-day working realities. It must be an evolving process in which everyone—including the CEO—can learn and relearn, question and answer, and, in the process, enact effective change. We must also recognize that mistakes are an important part of learning.

Unfortunately, what all too often is provided in the quest for learning is the traditional training program focused on quantitative outcomes—money spent, number of people trained, number of training hours delivered—rather than on qualitative measures—whether employees learn what they need to learn, whether behaviors are changed, and whether greater responsibility is accepted and sought.

This error—mistaking training programs for learning—stems directly from the failure of executives to articulate the role of true learning in their companies and a tendency to underestimate the value of learning as a tool in developing the business. Lacking clear direction, corporate training programs concentrate on feel-good efforts to provide traditional (read "classroom") courses addressing quick fixes of isolated problems.

Developing Employees Who Love to Learn provides a clear road map for how to avoid these mistakes and create successful learning in an organization. I suspect that most of what Linda Honold recommends will likely become standard practice in the future. Her ideas will gain important footholds because they revolve around the concept of learning rather than training. In this book, Linda presents a new focus on results-oriented training of human performance. She moves beyond traditional training methods to seize the opportunity to integrate training with an overarching imperative to allow people to develop themselves and achieve their true potential. The tools and strategies she offers are invigorating and can make the organizational heart beat faster.

I have great respect for Linda and her impressive successes with many companies. I first worked with her when she helped develop Johnsonville's approach to organizational learning as our first Member Development Coordinator and as my colleague in the Leadership Dynamics consulting group, spreading the message of change to other companies. A true lifelong learner, Linda carries those views, observations, and principles one step further by outlining a comprehensive approach to training and development that challenges traditional practices.

She doesn't stop with just challenging old ways. She specifies in considerable detail what kinds of practices should be developed and adopted. Her easy-to-implement methods of incorporating learning into day-to-day operations are important means for organizations to become more competitive in the 21st-century business environment. The reader should find the considerable detail about specific practices very helpful.

One of the great strengths of this book is that the author does not take a one-size-fits-all approach to training. She recognizes the diversity of ways in which individuals and organizations learn and the appropriateness of those organizations developing their own unique style befitting their culture and workplace environment. She also recognizes that learning and relearning is and needs to be continuous.

This book will help you. It should be read by everyone who is interested in transforming his or her organization by developing the talents of its people. It is written for leaders in any and all functional areas and is designed as a practical tool for anyone who needs to train people but does not have the expertise of a professional trainer. This strategic resource will make your job easier by demonstrating how to use the tools of effective, work-based training. It is for any manager who believes in the power of human potential.

Helping human beings fulfill their potential is good business. Fostering an expectation of learning and growth can result in enormous rates of return. It can and does change lives. In our case, using these methods has allowed managers to make sound investment decisions, ensure that resources are applied to key areas of operational needs, and identify barriers that prevent skills from being applied. More important, the commitment to personal learning and development has instilled a mind-set of initiative, achievement, and confidence that can transform an entire company.

Learning is change. Making learning a way of life in any company's setting may mean radical change. In most cases it represents needed change. Unlocking the unrealized potential of employees can lead to unprecedented success. This book will help lead your organization in the right direction.

One of the early leaders of the empowerment movement, Ralph Stayer is CEO of Johnsonville Sausage of Kohler, Wisconsin, and managing partner of Leadership Dynamics, a consulting group that specializes in organizational change. The story of his pioneering transformation of Johnsonville into a company that never stops learning has been acclaimed by national business publications and is frequently used in major graduate-level business school programs.

Preface

If you want 1 year of prosperity—grow grain. If you want 10 years of prosperity—grow trees. If you want 100 years of prosperity—grow people.

CHINESE PROVERB

Throughout the past few decades, formalized training programs have dominated the field of learning in the workplace. Yet research shows that most learning does not take place in a formalized classroom setting, but informally, often as a matter of course, in daily events. Since organizations don't plan for this informal learning, they are often unaware of its value. *Developing Employees Who Love to Learn* addresses this often overlooked asset and presents a system that complements more traditional training by focusing on less formal means of learning.

Not a New Concept

Focusing on learning rather than training is not a new concept. In 1961, Carl Rogers proclaimed that anything of value cannot be taught. But most books take a narrow approach to this topic. They may identify one type of learning—such as action learning (Marquardt, 1999) or self-managed learning (Cunningham, 1999)—and explore it in depth. Or they may write from a broad theoretical perspective (Candy, 1991; Merriam and Caffarella, 1999). Much has been written about the learning organization. Most of this work has focused on systemic issues (Senge, 1990; Senge et al., 1994) and organizational issues (Dixon, 1994; Kline and Saunders, 1993; Nonaka and Takeuchi, 1995; Pedler, Burgoyne, and Boydell, 1991; Watkins and Marsick, 1993; Watkins and Marsick, 1996). Little has been written about how individuals can best respond to change through learning.

Who Should Read This Book

This book focuses on assisting human resources, training, and organization development staff in designing and implementing systems that facilitate learning. Many of the strategies may be practiced without external support and can also be helpful to individuals who are trying to manage their own workplace learning and to supervisors who want to assist employees in their departments.

Developing Employees Who Love to Learn begins with the premise that individual learning is critical to the future success of employees and their organizations. The reasons for this are well known—change has become a way of life in business today. Even if an organization is not planning to change, it must adapt to changes in its environment. The marketplace today is global; improvements in technology occur constantly. This book applies not only to companies that profess to be "learning organizations" but also to companies that are faced with continual change in technology and in the marketplace, and require people who can adapt to those changes.

The idea for this book originated in my work as Member Development Coordinator at Johnsonville Sausage in Sheboygan Falls, Wisconsin. Johnsonville Sausage was featured in Tom Peters's book *Thriving on Chaos* (1987) and in his best-selling videotape *The Leadership Alliance* (1988). My entire job description was to "get people into a learning mode." In referring to the employees, Ralph Stayer, the company CEO, said, "Their lifelong learning was to take directions and orders, not to be asked questions. I wanted to help people become the instrument of their own destiny" (Peters, 1987, p. 287). In describing my job, he told me, "I believe that every person truly wants to be great! We have a moral obligation to create an organization where people are allowed to develop to their full potential." Stayer wanted to make the company grow. Our underlying assumption was that people who are learning will be more open to change. We created opportunities for people to learn, grow, and develop themselves. As a result, the organization grew too. We went from a company that used people to grow a great business to a company that used the business to grow great people. In the end, we all won. Since that time, I have worked with many other companies toward a similar goal. This book is the culmination of those efforts and of research on companies that are engaged in workplace learning.

How the Book Is Organized

The book begins with a discussion of adult learning and the rationale for creating learning opportunities within organizations. It examines the development of a learning system and the support systems necessary to sustain it. The latter part of the book presents more specific applications.

Part 1 consists of three chapters: Chapter 1 proposes the general concept of individual learning from the perspectives of the organization, the individual, and the human resources, training, or organization development department. Chapter 2 discusses why an organization would want to spend time, money, and other resources on learning. Chapter 3 presents perspectives on adult learning. It describes four basic patterns that are used throughout the book to describe learning opportunities and will assist readers in selecting those that are most appropriate for their needs.

Part 2 addresses the development of a learning system. It discusses how to select those aspects of individual learning that are pertinent to your organization and how to develop an implementation plan. Chapter 4 describes the initiation, conceptualization, and planning phases. It suggests a process for identifying the underlying philosophy and creating a mission. It recommends ways in which to select the most appropriate ideas for an individual organization and mechanisms for developing a learning system plan. It also provides a worksheet for developing a complete learning system.

Chapter 5 discusses the development, implementation, and improvement of your learning system. Without these key elements, organizations cannot sustain learning. This chapter describes the support systems necessary to ensure that learning remains a vital part of your work environment; it also comments on the concept of creating a specific system for learning within today's organizations.

Part 3 offers a variety of ways to develop and sustain individual and group learning. Chapter 6 outlines tools for entering into a learning mode, including Personal Development Workshops aimed at assisting individuals in determining their goals, learning styles, decision-making approaches, values, and so on. Chapter 7 provides suggestions for ongoing individual learning. Chapter 8 focuses on methods of learning while working with another person, such as mentoring, employee interaction, and peer dyads or triads. It emphasizes the need to make learning explicit when working in pairs and suggests strategies for integrating peer learning into your employees' daily work.

Chapter 9 discusses how to focus on individual learning while working in a group or team. It includes learning sets (Cunningham, Bennett, and Dawes, 2000), reflective meeting notes (Castleberg, 1999), reading groups, business plan development, and customer champions. Chapter 10 discusses ways of integrating individual learning with group performance. Chapter 11 discusses the role of the manager and supervisor in facilitating learning in the workplace.

Format

Part 3 offers a collection of ideas. Not all of the suggestions will appeal to every reader or be applicable to every organization, nor is it possible to implement all the suggestions simultaneously. While it is important to create an overall plan, you may work on any particular aspect that suits you at any given time, then move on to experiment with another idea.

What works for one organization may not work for another. So the ideas are offered as concepts rather than as part of a recipe or formula. I suggest ways in which organizations may use them but leave creation of the learning opportunity to each individual company. Wherever possible, I have listed references that will provide for additional information about a particular idea.

A Personal Note

For much of my working life, I have struggled with the relationships between education, training, career development, and learning to learn, or developing the skills for acquiring knowledge. I attended a high school and participated in doctoral programs that were based on the premise that people really want to learn and can be responsible for their own learning; their systems were structured to reinforce that belief. The last 15 years of my career have been dedicated largely to learning in the workplace. I have collected ideas and data from a variety of organizations and share these experiences in this book. If you believe your experiences would contribute to the generation of learning and would like others to know about them, please feel free to contact me at lhonold@execpc.com.

About the Author

Linda Honold, Ph.D., is a human resource development and organization consultant focusing on the topic of creating opportunities for employee learning. She is the former Coach for Member Development at Johnsonville Sausage, the company that was featured in Tom Peters's best-selling book *Thriving on Chaos* and his videotape *The Leadership Alliance*. Honold is a member of OD Network, Academy of Management, and American Society for Training and Development.

INDIVIDUAL LEARNING
IN THE WORKPLACE

In order to have a world-class company and workforce, corporate America must create and foster an environment where there is continuous learning, training, alignment of strategic goals, and knowledge-sharing through the company. In doing so, it helps to create and prepare workers to assume more responsibilities and solve problems themselves. They need this to remain competitive in the industry.

MICHAEL A. JOHNSTON
Chairman, Merrill Lynch Credit Corporation
1997 Malcolm Baldrige National Quality Award Winner

Why would an organization want to invest time, money, and effort in the creation of an individual learning system? What is the return for the organization? What is the benefit for individuals? Chapter 1 describes the distinctive characteristics of individual learning in the workplace.

Chapter 2 explains why it is worthwhile to invest time, money, and energy in individual learning—taking into account the perspectives of the organization, the individual, and the human resources, training, or organization development department.

Chapter 3 presents approaches to adult learning and shows how they apply to the practice of individual learning set forth in this book. Readers who are interested in immediately applying tools and strategies for learning and those who are already familiar with adult learning theory may be tempted to bypass this discussion, but I recommend that these readers at least skim through this chapter, for several reasons. They may be interested in anecdotes that illustrate the application of these approaches to organizational life. New concepts about learning in organizations establish the groundwork for discussions of various learning processes in Part 3. These concepts are essential to understanding the creation of an organizational learning system and also provide context for the later sections of the book.

Characteristics of Learning in Organizations

In a world that is constantly changing, there is not one subject or set of subjects that will serve you for the foreseeable future, let alone for the rest of your life. The most important skill to acquire now is learning how to learn.

JOHN NAISBITT

Learning occurs everywhere in organizations—wherever employees face problems, deal with unforeseen issues, or maneuver their way around obstacles to get their work done. As much as 70% of learning at work is done outside the classroom in an informal setting (U.S. Department of Labor, 1996). The real issue is whether the individuals and organizations involved are capitalizing on the opportunity so that it will be of value in the future.

Why Focus on Learning?

"Everyone will increasingly be expected not only to be good at something, to have their own professional or technical expertise, but will also very rapidly acquire responsibility for money, people, projects, or all three—a managerial task, in other words" (Handy, 1989). As this quote notes, the marketplace is continually changing. Information and data are instantaneously available. The market is no longer local, it is global. Competition is fierce. Organizations must adapt in order to survive, and the people within them must change to meet new demands. Peter Vaill (1989) compares the old economic system to navigating a canoe that is floating down a gently flowing river. The manager's job was to guide the canoe and provide direction for the paddlers. As long as the workers continued to paddle—to do their jobs as they were told—things were fine. Today's world of business management, he continues, is more like navigating continual white-water rapids. It takes more than managers making decisions and working toward improvement. Every person in the company must, at times, act like a manager. All employees contribute to keeping up with the marketplace. Sometimes this means involvement in decision making. At other times, employees must be willing to implement changes recommended by management.

important concept

How can employees become engaged in such activities? They must see that being engaged is part of their role. It doesn't work to simply tell an employee, "You need to act like a manager," or, "You must be open to change." Engagement cannot be forced. Both skills and attitudes are at issue. While decision-making skills can be taught, attitudes cannot. Attitudes come from within individuals and can only be changed by the individuals themselves. They must truly understand the idea and feel a sense of ownership toward it.

The best way to achieve such a state is to have a workforce filled with learners. Why? Learning and change are synonymous. One cannot change without learning something; one cannot learn without changing something, even if it is only a mental process. The challenge is to get people to learn. Since people engage in learning anyway, this doesn't appear to be an overwhelming task. It is not, however, as straightforward as it seems.

Ask people what they have learned lately and they will invariably tell you about the last class or most recent training program they attended. Attending a class or being in a training program does not necessarily mean that anything was learned. It is natural for people to think learning takes place only in a formal classroom setting. From childhood on, most of us went to school to learn. We are unlikely to describe as learning something that occurred informally on the job, in a conversation with a peer or mentor, or in a recently read book. Yet most learning takes place in these settings. A formal approach may be best for some people or for certain subjects, but not for all situations. An expert on self-managed learning, Ian Cunningham (1999) suggests that "people learn most often from sources other than courses."

Characteristics of Learning in the Workplace

Learning in the workplace may occur in a planned training environment or spontaneously, as employees are challenged on the job to achieve a production goal or to come up with a customer-demanded product improvement. Learning in the workplace includes the following key concepts:

- Responsibility for learning resides with the learner

- Learning begins with knowledge about self

- Learning occurs just in time for use

- Learning requires flexibility in setting

- Solutions are not necessarily known

- Learning requires flexibility in approaches

- New learning often involves unlearning

- Learning is integrated with work

- Learning is a conscious process

Responsibility for Learning Resides with the Learner

People who have been taught may not know how to learn. In classrooms and in many training programs, teachers are responsible for determining the content of the material they present. They impart this information to those who are there to learn. In a more self-directed type of learning, the learner has responsibility for his or her own learning. Often the learner determines what is to be learned. The teacher is generally less a presenter of knowledge than a facilitator who involves the learner in the process of locating resources through which to learn. Sometimes the content focuses on attaining the skills and knowledge to achieve organizational goals. At other times, personal issues are stressed, as they are critical to engaging the individual in learning.

For example, Chaparral Steel needed to increase the yield on a specific lathe in order to meet the needs of its customers (Solomon, 1994).

A manager asked the machinist who operated the lathe to investigate the purchase of another one in order to meet the need. The operator visited companies that used the lathe in the United States as well as in Japan. He then selected a used machine rather than a brand-new one and saved the company $300,000. This is an example of workplace learning. Had the manager done the same investigation and come to the same conclusion, it is likely the machine operator would have grumbled about being given secondhand equipment. Instead, the lathe operator not only learned a great deal about the equipment's cost and operation but also gained a stake in making the new machine function effectively. And the manager learned about the capabilities of the employee.

Learning is accessible to all employees in an organization, not just to managers or those who are seen by management as in need of upgrading their skills. As Vaill (1989) indicated, all employees must work to meet organizational objectives and must change in one way or another—therefore all employees must be learning.

Learning Begins with Knowledge About Self

Operating under the assumption that all learning is relevant, both formal and informal, Argyris (1993) observes that "success in the marketplace increasingly depends on learning, yet most people don't know how to learn" (p. 177). Most people do not know which learning methods work best for them. They have not purposefully thought about what they would like to learn or why they would like to learn it. Being a learner requires self-examination and an understanding of one's own learning style, values, belief, and interests. Then the learning process becomes much more effective. The *Myers-Briggs Type Indicator*® instrument can help people learn about themselves and how they relate to others.

Susan, a human resources manager, knew that she was uncomfortable around people she did not know or if she did not have business to conduct. She found engaging in small talk stressful because she could never think of what to say. Given that she really enjoyed working with people at her job, she could not understand why she felt this way.

Susan had the opportunity to take the *Myers-Briggs Type Indicator*® instrument in a class she attended. When she received the results, she saw, among other things, that she was a strong introvert. She learned that introversion in this context did not mean shy and reserved, but instead described the way she oriented herself to the world. As she explored this issue more deeply, she realized that her discomfort disappeared when she talked about topics that were of interest to others or to herself. Susan learned to ask other people about their hobbies and interests, which got conversations going and eased her discomfort.

By achieving a deeper insight into herself, Susan was able to develop the skills to address difficult situations. As she continued her self-exploration, she developed more learning skills. She was also able to relate her increased understanding of herself to the differences she saw in others, thereby advancing her understanding of them as well.

Learning Occurs Just in Time for Use

Learning generally does not follow a logical sequence. It happens when it happens—in a classroom, while reflecting on an experience, or in the midst of a conversation with another person. It takes place when the learner needs it and at a location that fits the need.

A manufacturing plant manager received a page summoning him to the company's parking lot. There, he was confronted with an expensive forklift lying on its side on the pavement. He learned that the shipping department's forklift had been malfunctioning. An employee from that department called the receiving department to see if he could borrow one, promising that he would get it back as soon as possible. The facility was large and sprawling. The employee decided that the best way to transport the forklift to his area was by loading it onto a truck and driving it through the parking lot. He was trying to finish his chore as quickly as possible and did not take the time to secure the forklift to the flatbed truck he was using to transport it. While he was rounding a turn in the parking lot, the forklift rolled off the truck and landed on its side.

The plant manager assessed the situation; he looked at the forklift, the truck, and then the employee. He shook his head and asked, "So, what have you learned from this?" He helped the employee think through what had happened, and why, and together they developed an alternative strategy should a similar situation present itself in the future. The manager could have yelled at the employee or invoked the company's disciplinary policy. Both actions probably would have upset the employee, and he might have ended up carrying a chip on his shoulder.

The manager knew this was an accident, not a purposeful act. By asking the employee what he had learned from the situation and helping him think it through, the plant manager turned this mishap into an opportunity for learning rather than blame.

＊Mistakes can be a valuable learning tool. In this case, learning took place at the time of the incident, with experience and the manager acting as the teacher.

Learning Requires Flexibility in Setting

People naturally tend to look for a class to fill a learning need. This is not always the best approach. Learning does not necessarily require a formal setting. In organizations, it requires the creation of spaces and opportunities for people to learn.

At the conclusion of a learning-to-learn workshop, a facilitator was counseling an individual who had identified a desire to become a packaging engineer. The learner was discouraged because there were no suitable programs within 150 miles of his home. He could not afford to quit work to attend school. The facilitator and the learner talked about why he wanted to learn packaging engineering and found that his interest stemmed from his position as a supervisor in a packaging department. He really did not need a degree; he just wanted to enhance his working knowledge. Further, when they considered his learning style, they found that he learned primarily through conversation with others, followed closely by a "learn by doing" approach.

As they looked around the community where he lived, they found that there were several packaging engineers at other companies. The learner contacted these individuals, talked with them, and eventually found one with whom he felt comfortable. They established a mentoring-type relationship that fulfilled the learner's need without requiring him to quit work to go to school.

In this case, learning took place in an informal setting—with the aid of both the learning facilitator and the engineer/mentor—which created a more conducive individual learning situation. In order for novice learners to incorporate new approaches to learning, some facilitation by a learning professional will likely be required—as this kind of flexibility is a new way of thinking about learning.

Solutions Are Not Necessarily Known

Creating opportunities for learning in organizations is different from developing training programs. Training generally assists in addressing known issues. A trainer, who already has the relevant skill or knowledge, assists the learner in acquiring the same ability or information. In today's rapidly changing environment, we cannot predict all of the issues that may confront us.

For instance, a machine operator was asked by a salesperson if his machine could wrap a package that was $2^1/2$ inches wide and 5 inches long. The machine normally wrapped packages that were at least 8 inches long and 6 inches wide. The operator went to the company engineers to ask what they thought. While the engineers did not know the answer, they were able to provide the operator with a contact at the company that manufactured the machine. The manufacturer's engineers told the operator that such a small package could not be wrapped with the current equipment and that his company would have to purchase a different machine. The machine operator thought about the problem overnight. He went to work early the next day and began reconfiguring the machine. With a little experimentation he was able to meet the salesperson's wrapping specifications. The solution to this problem was not known; it was discovered through experimentation.

Learning becomes part of everyone's job. People must be able to adapt. Employees need to extend what they already know and apply it to new situations. When the solution to a problem cannot be taught because it is unknown, learning often takes place through active experimentation.

Learning Requires Flexibility in Approaches

Sometimes learning occurs by reading, sometimes by reflecting, other times by experimentation, and now and then by doing something that seems a bit bizarre. Learning approaches must incorporate flexibility.

One day, the plant coordinator of a Johnsonville Sausage plant instructed all of the core team members to jump into a van and go grocery shopping. (Plant coordinators differ from plant managers in that they see their role as coordinating activities and developing people rather than managing a facility. Core team members coordinate the activities of various shifts at a plant.) In this case, the core team members were looking for products manufactured at their plant as well as those made by their competitors. The company was anticipating a cyclical slowdown in sales during the winter season. The group was looking for better ways to utilize their assets in the off-season. As they combed through the grocery store shelves and talked about the differences in product packaging and display, they realized that two of their major competitors offered a type of product that they were not making. They checked with the sales and marketing staff and the research and development team. Johnsonville Sausage then decided to produce the item the following season. As it turned out, customers really liked the new product. The company also found a whole new market for the product that the competition had not yet discovered. Sales were much greater than anticipated in the first year and quadrupled in the next.

A system of individual learning does not have to be located in any one place. It can take place anywhere, for anyone, but it almost always involves critical thinking skills. In the above case, the plant leadership group had to be thinking about what was not present on the grocery shelves as well as about what was there. The learning process stemmed from the question "What needs to be done to get from where we are to where we need to be?"

New Learning Often Involves Unlearning

Sometimes learning something new means we must accept the concept of unlearning. We may have learned something a certain way and believe it is the absolute truth. As we become learners, we discover that frequently there is more than one truth. When we look at things from a different perspective, another truth reveals itself.

The chief executive officer of a corporation was trying to change his management style. When employees came to him with problems, he tended to respond by telling them what to do. He knew that by giving them the answers, he was not really helping them because they would always expect someone else to solve their problems for them. The CEO was trying to do a better job of developing people by asking them questions that would help them think through the issues and make their own decisions.

After numerous failed attempts, he decided to tape-record himself in meetings. The idea was not to hear what others said but to catch himself giving answers. After listening to the tapes, the CEO tried to think of different ways to respond. Over time, he learned to ask questions instead of giving answers. He also succeeded in helping his employees develop new abilities. The tape recordings enabled the CEO to unlearn his typical response to a specific situation so he could learn a new approach.

Learning Is Integrated with Work

While some learning takes place as a separate activity, much can occur during the process of getting the job done.

In the early 1980s, a company opened a packaging facility where they custom made plastic wrapping and wrapped products for their clients. This facility was created to fill an existing need—the market was already there and products were immediately in demand. As a result, there was not a great deal of time available for training new employees on new equipment. People had to learn how to operate the equipment as they went along. Over time, the operators became experts on their equipment.

Today the company is growing. New operators are being hired and trained. The longer-term employees are of the opinion that something has happened to the labor pool. The newer ones "just aren't of the same caliber." Or "they just don't seem to be able to learn the machinery." On further examination, it becomes clear that whenever there is a problem with the equipment, the newer operators go to the seasoned operators, who fix the problem. There is no learning involved. The newer operators are frustrated because the older ones will not teach them the tricks of the trade. The older ones are equally frustrated because the newer ones just are not learning it—"even after we've told them half a dozen times."

Allowing seasoned operators to make all of the decisions has made the organization more efficient in some respects. In other ways, though, the company has lost a great deal. The new employees do not learn anything when the longer-term employees fix all the problems. The challenge is to find a happy medium, where work gets done but new employees are able to learn about the job and internalize their understanding of the process. If the veteran operators learn to help their newer coworkers solve problems themselves as difficulties occur, both groups will benefit from the shared experience, and the company will have more employees with the skills they need to do their jobs.

Learning Is a Conscious Process

Effective learning for people and organizations requires an awareness of the process as an option. If learning is not consciously chosen, it is often accidental and inefficient. A person may learn something new and not even realize it. Conscious learning means that employees are in a learning mode, know that the responsibility for learning is with the learner, and understand that, over time, learning becomes more self-directed.

Being in a learning mode enables people to embrace change. The organization, then, will have more learners if it creates a series of mechanisms, or a system, for learning. When employees are responsible for learning, they become more conscious of it. Rather than relying on someone else to teach them, they begin to recognize that they need additional skills and knowledge to make decisions. They seek out learning opportunities instead of waiting for someone else to provide them. This is what we mean by self-directed learning.

If change is constant for organizations, it is also ever present for individuals, who must adapt to change if they are to thrive. If they cannot adapt rapidly, they and their organization may fall behind in the marketplace. Self-directed learners tend to work on their learning independently and have the persistence to stay with the process. They also tend to see problems as challenges, be goal-directed, explore alternative learning activities, and decide on priorities.

In this chapter, we have begun to develop an understanding of workplace learning. In Chapter 2, we will explore the benefits of developing a workplace environment conducive to ongoing self-directed learning.

Realizing the Power
of Individual Learning

Learning is the most powerful, engaging, rewarding and enjoyable aspect of our personal and collective experience. The ability
to learn about learning and become masters of the learning
process is critical for the next century.

JOHN BURGOYNE ET AL.
A Declaration on Learning

Individual learning in organizations provides benefits to many
of the major stakeholders: the organization itself; the people involved;
and the staff of the human resources development, training, or organization development department—even society as a whole. To gain the
most benefit, it is important to understand the potential value of this
often spontaneous phenomenon.

Making the Most of Your Internal Labor Market

"Investment in continuous learning has been critical to achieving our
vision. Most important, it has reinforced that people are our most important asset, produced a highly motivated team, and increased the level of
service to our customers," says Ed Schultz, Chairman of Dana
Commercial Credit Corporation (quoted in U.S. Department of
Commerce, 1999, p. 13). Learning is imperative in the workplace if an
organization wants to increase its productivity.

Beyond the organization's need, learning is critical because companies now employ a different type of worker. Production workers, while
still a major component of the labor force, have been partially replaced
by knowledge workers—employees who use their minds more than their

hands. These employees represent intellectual capital. As the world keeps changing, knowledge workers must add to what they know in order to stay current or ahead of the competition. The vice president of an organization affected by a change in its internal labor market was well aware of this fact when she stated to a new employee, "As of today, all your current knowledge is becoming obsolete. We hired you with the knowledge you have—it is your responsibility to continually upgrade it."

There are a number of significant organizational and individual benefits from engaging in learning at the workplace. Among these benefits are

- Increased productivity and quality

- Increased innovation

- Increased adaptability to change

- Competitive advantage

- Fewer barriers to communication

- Increased employee attraction and retention

- Increased employee motivation

- Increased benefit from education/training dollars

- Integration of learning into work

Benefits to the organization begin with bottom-line productivity and expand to include the ability to attract and retain employees and an increased return on investments in training and education. Workplace learning also satisfies the more humanistic moral imperative of allowing people to grow and develop. It is a strategic investment, both for the organization and for the development of human capital.

Increased Productivity and Quality

A major reason for creating learning systems is to promote productivity. Although books describe individual learning and show organizations how to generate strategies for planned learning and human resources development (Argyris and Schön, 1974; Cunningham, 1999), workplace learning has received relatively little attention as a tool for increasing productivity and quality. Yet innovative companies have been purposefully implementing learning opportunities for at least 15 years. These forward-looking organizations understand that when people are learning, there are significant positive increases in their performance and the quality of the products or services they provide.

Organizational investment in equipment can result in a limited amount of productivity improvement. It has been demonstrated that increases in worker knowledge increase productivity by as much as 16% (Lynch and Black, 1996). On average, a 10% increase in the value of capital equipment leads to a .75% increase in productivity; the same 10% increase in workforce education leads to an 8.6% productivity gain (Lynch and Black, 1996). Learning can become part of an organization's competitive advantage. If learning is viewed as an investment that leads to a payoff, rather than as a cost to be written off, the benefits translate into bottom-line results.

When Chaparral Steel began implementing learning processes, it produced 1 ton of steel for approximately every 2.5 to 3 employee-hours. The company has now reduced production time to 1 ton for approximately every 1.5 employee-hours (Solomon, 1994). Bostrom Seating implemented a learning system with a goal of improving quality as well as its workforce. It credits its learning system for a 38% reduction in in-house quality problems, a 31% reduction in quality problems discovered by its customers, and an 8% decrease in appraisal costs (Millner et al., 1999). For both of these companies, improvement in the bottom line and in quality is obvious. Learning can also lead to increased innovation.

Increased Innovation

Employees who are learning are more inclined to innovate particularly when encouraged by the organization. This enhances a producer's or service provider's ability to be responsive to the needs of its customers. United Technologies (McCain and Pantazis, 1997) and 3M (Brand, 1998) both claim that their learning systems have a positive impact on innovation. To encourage innovation, they make room for it and provide systems to reinforce it. Innovation can also improve in-house functions.

Management staff at a manufacturing facility were struggling with a lack of warehouse space. They came up with a short-term solution of temporarily shipping their finished goods to a warehouse owned by another company several miles away. When it was time to deliver the product to their customers, the goods were transferred back and stored briefly in their on-site warehouse. This process was extremely costly—in both time and money. Management of the company knew they would not have the financial capital to construct a new warehouse for at least three years.

A cross-functional team of department managers who were being affected by the situation began looking into various options for dealing with the dilemma. They came up with an innovative idea. They located an individual who wanted to expand his business but could not afford to build a second warehouse. If the company in need of warehouse space agreed to lease half of a new facility, he would build it on the company's land. He could then afford to develop additional clients for his half of the facility. With the profits from his new customers, the warehouser would be able to build a facility on his own land, and, at the end of five years, the manufacturing company could purchase the warehouse for itself. This win-win solution would not have been possible without the manufacturing company's learning-oriented, experimental approach.

Increased Adaptability to Change

"The new jobs in tomorrow's industries, in manufacturing and services alike, will call for more than button-pressing automatons. They will require workers that are literate, numerate, adaptable, and trainable" (Anonymous, 1997, p. 17). One of the best ways to develop a more adaptable workforce is to employ people who learn. Learning and change are virtually synonymous. Therefore, if employees are learning, they are more open to change.

A production worker in a factory was known as one of the biggest grumblers in the plant. He never seemed to be happy with change implemented in the company. An informational brochure was posted on the bulletin board announcing a new educational program that would help employees understand the workings of the whole company. The grumbling production worker signed up for the course.

Over the next year, this learning group met every other week for three hours. At each session, they learned about one aspect of the company. Everything from the company's mission, to the profit-and-loss statement, to production and sales were described by managers from the various units.

Additional educational components included a session on giving a presentation. Each participant was required to make a 15-minute presentation during the final weeks of the program. Much to everyone's surprise, the grumbler, who had been viewed as quite negative, decided to give his presentation on teamwork. It was so well done that some of his colleagues asked him to make the presentation at their team meeting. The learning opportunity led to a real change in this individual. He became one of the positive-opinion leaders in his department.

Competitive Advantage

Maintaining an organization filled with people who are learning creates a competitive advantage. In addition to increasing productivity and enhancing the ability to adapt quickly to a changing environment, you will eventually be employing more knowledgeable, valuable people than your competitors are. Investing in your employees' learning results in a strategic competitive advantage.

The management at a manufacturing company chose to develop systems for learning in conjunction with a structural shift toward a team-based organization. They achieved marked success in their efforts and gained some acclaim in the business press. In examining their situation, their major competitor determined that the primary cause of the improvement was the use of teams. So the competitor company set about creating teams as well, but, when the teams did not produce the desired results, it reverted to its traditional structure. In trying to emulate the success of its competitor, the company failed to realize the importance of the learning component. Simply installing teams did not generate employees who could provide a competitive advantage.

When learning assists in aligning employees with corporate goals, performance levels rise. After employees get into the learning mode, most of their learning helps align them with corporate goals. Employees' learning is a strategic investment that cannot be replicated. Technology can be reproduced, but your workforce cannot. Your employees are your only long-term competitive advantage. Investment in learning increases that advantage.

Fewer Barriers to Communication

Middle management has often functioned as an information gatekeeper. Part of its role has been to transfer information from higher management to frontline employees. As communication technology makes information more universally accessible, this role becomes less critical. As employees learn more, middle managers become mentors and teachers. They help employees to better understand the additional information—how it fits into their jobs, their departments, and the overall strategic plan of the company. This results in a new type of relationship and fewer misunderstandings from lack of communication.

Jack Stack, CEO of Springfield Remanufacturing, describes a process in which managers are conveyors of information and providers of education (Stack, 1992). Each week, supervisors aggregate their unit's production numbers and report them to the production manager. Early in the week, management team members report data from their areas of responsibility at a pre–staff meeting. Each line of the facility's profit-and-loss statement is filled in by the person responsible for that item. Production members sometimes attend the first meeting as part of their education process. This enables them to see what happens to the numbers they generate and provide to their supervisor for use at the pre–staff meeting.

A staff meeting takes place every other Wednesday morning. All corporate staff, the general manager of each division, and other divisional members attend as needed, either to provide input or at their request. Each line of the profit-and-loss statement is filled in for each unit of the company. Using a laptop computer, a spreadsheet program, and a data projector, this financial information is projected onto a large screen so that it is visible to all.

Within 48 hours of the staff meeting, managers get together with their departments. The supervisors then meet with department production members. The opening phase is generally educational. The division accountant leads a practical discussion about some aspect of the financial statement. Post–staff meetings conclude with reviews of financial results for both company and division, any pertinent announcements, and a question-and-answer period.

In this process, the company not only keeps track of its weekly performance, it shares information with every person—with managers and supervisors serving as the communicators. This process also educates all employees about the company's overall financial situation.

Increased Employee Attraction and Retention

In a time of low unemployment, attracting good employees is often a daunting task. An emphasis on learning tends to attract high-quality employees who are inclined toward continually developing themselves. This kind of person prefers an organization that actively encourages and provides opportunities for learning. As well as attracting employees, learning is a tool for retaining employees.

The cost of replacing employees is high. The turnover cost for one machinist in a precision machine shop may run as high as $20,000, taking into account the separation costs of an exit interview, administrative record keeping, advertising, interviewing, training, and lost productivity due to the reduced efficiency caused by a new machinist and mistakes made during training (Mercer, 1989; 1993).

A purchasing manager at a manufacturing company that incorporates learning and growth in its work processes had the goal of becoming a vice president. He knew such an opportunity was not likely with his current employer, so when he heard of an opening with a nearby organization, he applied for the job and was hired. Within two months, he called his former employer and asked if the company would consider hiring him back. He had gotten his title, but the new company's philosophy was that learning takes place before entering the workplace. He realized there was greater value in continued learning than in having the title of vice president.

Formal and informal learning transforms mobile workers into more stable ones (Davenport, 1999). Because much learning occurs on the job, workplace learning leads to increased engagement. Learning builds commitment toward the organization and often loyalty. Most organizations today do not want people who just come in, do their jobs, and go home. They want people who can recognize a problem, identify it, bring it to management's attention, and perhaps help to resolve it.

Increased Employee Motivation

John Adair (1999), a United Kingdom–based author on leadership, proposes that 50% of employees' motivation is internal; the other 50% is created elsewhere. He suggests that while one person cannot directly motivate another, one of the primary ways to affect motivation is to create a learning environment.

good concept

Pay, recognition, and other forms of incentive are extrinsic motivators—they come from outside the individual. Once a person learns to learn, the learning itself becomes an intrinsic motivator. Douglas McGregor (1960) answers the question "How do you motivate people?" by saying that you don't. Rather, you create a context in which they motivate themselves because they have opportunities to be engaged in their work—to learn. Quality-management guru W. Edwards Deming (Bennis and Schein, 1966) echoes McGregor's comment.

Through learning, companies can provide processes and systems to intrinsically motivated people. This does not mean that pay is not important. As Frederick Herzberg (1968) found, pay does not motivate people, but low pay can be a demotivator. An unfair compensation can detract from productivity and quality. Intrinsic rewards do not replace the more traditional financial rewards, but they can enhance them.

Once a person engages in conscious learning, it often becomes addictive. It is the potato chip phenomenon—once you have tried learning, you cannot stop with just a single experience. It becomes a way of life. Absenteeism may decline as a result of increased motivation because people find more value in their work.

A factory that invested in employee development posted a signboard to greet visitors in the lobby. One day, when there were no guests scheduled, the employee responsible for putting up the greeting posted the words "Welcome—Thank Goodness It's Monday." This employee actually looked forward to coming to work because of the opportunities for learning, growth, and development.

Increased Benefit from Education/Training Dollars

This chapter cites many examples of learning that occurs during the work process, not apart from it. Workplace learning is often integrated with and applies directly to the job. It is easy to recognize its value. It is inexpensive because it frequently occurs naturally, without formal instruction. When people learn from and with one another in their workplaces and on the job, the result may be a great deal of learning with no need for tuition or books.

Integration of Learning into Work

One of the most difficult challenges for trainers is figuring out how to transfer information imparted in the classroom into the workplace. Consciously designed learning systems that exist alongside real work systems increase employees' ability to integrate learning into their jobs.

Benefits for the Individual

The following story about Paul, a motor-coach driver, may illustrate the potential benefits of learning for individual development. Each week, Paul leaves his home in Christchurch, New Zealand, to drive a busload of tourists through the mountains to Queenstown. The next morning, he transports another group of tourists to the Franz Joseph Glacier. On the third day, he drives his passengers to Greymouth, where they ride a train through the Southern Alps while he drives to the Christchurch train station. There he picks them up, and conveys them to their hotels. He repeats this trip week after week.

You might think a job like this would become routine at some point. But Paul's weekly trip is anything but routine. On any given day, there could be passengers from the United States, England, Japan, Canada, Australia, Sweden, and/or Germany. Paul makes a point of asking his passengers about their cultures and home countries. He has become well versed in the differences between the various countries. Sometimes Paul drives for groups that are studying nature or geology. He studies right along with them. His newfound knowledge becomes potential topics of conversation with future passengers. Paul is continually learning.

The World Initiative on Lifelong Learning suggests that learning become a "continuously supportive process that stimulates and empowers individuals to acquire all the knowledge, values, skills, and understanding they will require throughout their lifetimes and to apply them with confidence, creativity, and enjoyment in all roles, circumstances, and environments" (Stewart and Ball, 1995, p. 5). Over time, learning becomes a benefit similar to other forms of indirect compensation for individuals engaged in learning. For example, a union worker discovered that "there is freedom in education—freedom to pursue a better job, freedom to realize our potential" (Goldberg, 1999).

Houle (1961) identified three types of learners: goal-oriented, activity-oriented, and learning-oriented.

- *Goal-oriented* learners use learning to achieve a goal. Like the individual who wanted to learn about packaging engineering, these learners are often responding to external expectations for continuing education and professional advancement—or perhaps to the need to serve others.

- *Activity-oriented* learners are interested in the activity of learning. It may augment social interaction, provide escape from boredom, or, as in the motor-coach driver's case, constitute a means of personal stimulation.

- *Learning-oriented* learners are those who seek knowledge for its own sake, such as the employee who devised the "Thank Goodness It's Monday" sign. Learning becomes valuable because learners enjoy it.

Organizations that provide systems for learning address the needs of all three types of learners.

The list below shows potential benefits to the individual for engaging in learning.

- More interesting work

- Discovery of career direction

- Understanding of personal values

- Universal accessibility

- Personal satisfaction

- Joy of achievement

- Enhanced employment security

- Employability

- Increased wages

More Interesting Work

Learning makes work more interesting. Instead of approaching work as if it were a routine chore, the same thing week after week, Paul, the motor-coach driver, turned his job into his own personal classroom. Learning can contribute to the continuous flow of new ideas and make workdays interesting. It can also lead to self-fulfillment and personal growth. On a more practical level, learning can help people find and keep satisfying jobs.

Discovery of Career Direction

By early adulthood, some people know what they want to do in their careers. A good many do not. We leave school and enter the workforce, taking whatever job is available or appeals to us. At some point, we may realize that, if we had a choice, we would choose another occupation. Sometimes those who were certain about their career from early adulthood find after they have been working for a while that the job is no longer fulfilling, or their employer may downsize or eliminate their position.

Some organizations have created employee work-along days, when workers from anywhere in the company can spend a day in another department. In one such company, over a period of several months, a factory worker spent a day in sales, a day in shipping, and a day in customer service. She determined that the company was lacking some essential communication. People in one department didn't know what those in other departments were doing. This led to confusion about new products and miscommunication between departments—despite the time spent preparing interdepartmental reports—which lowered customer confidence in the company. With the assistance of her manager, the employee formulated a job description and a plan for a new liaison position that would facilitate the flow of information and result in internal and external satisfaction. Through a learning system designed to help employees understand the company, this employee discovered a problem and created a solution that allowed her to grow while it also served organizational goals.

Understanding of Personal Values

Knowing oneself and one's own personal values is critical to becoming a versatile, effective, self-managed learner. Many people have never thought about their own personal values, or the reasons behind their beliefs. After engaging in this kind of self-exploration, a person becomes more familiar with his or her own personal value system and develops a deeper awareness about his or her choices in life.

This process helped one worker understand why, despite better pay and benefits, and pressure from friends, she chose not to accept a job offer from another company. She came to understand that loyalty was an important value for her. Her present employer had always treated her well and stood by her when she experienced some personal difficulties. Others thought the difference in pay and benefits should be enough to break that bond. After all, they reasoned, she had stayed with the company for five years after it helped her out. The workplace is an economic exchange, they told her, and she should take the better opportunity. Yet she was still uncomfortable about leaving. Once she realized the personal value she attached to loyalty, she understood why it was so important to her to stay.

Universal Accessibility

As we have seen, learning enables employees to respond more quickly to changing circumstances, which are inevitable in today's fast-paced, global business world. Learning is not just for knowledge workers—individuals in managerial, administrative, professional, technical, and sales jobs. It is also critical for production and service workers. When everyone in the organization benefits from learning, the organization benefits as well.

Personal Satisfaction

Abraham Maslow (1943) told us about the human needs of safety and security, belonging, status, and self-actualization. Learning can be a mechanism for fulfilling some psychological needs. Among the possible benefits from learning are

- Achieving a goal

- Developing social connections and friendships

- Experiencing the joy of seeking knowledge for its own sake

- Meeting organizational expectations for learning, which may be necessary for professional advancement. Even if learning is not required, it may lead to career advancement.

- Meeting individual altruistic desires by helping others to learn or by serving the community

- Turning work into a learning activity, to enrich routines and eliminate boredom

- Improving self-esteem, as people who are learning tend to feel better about themselves

In learning, an employee can achieve a stronger sense of personal accomplishment and satisfaction. Employees may undertake learning for their own benefit. The benefit to the organization is icing on the cake.

Joy of Achievement

Learning often leads to a higher level of development than does training. People who advance to higher levels of development are better able to manage their own learning.

A young employee at a manufacturing organization entered the workforce immediately after high school graduation. He began on the factory floor in an entry-level position and, because he showed promise, was able to move into a more technically sophisticated position. His employer was located in a rural area and maintained its own wastewater treatment plant. The treatment plant operator accepted another position with the company, and the young worker applied for and was awarded the job at the treatment plant. The young man worked with the experienced operator until the older employee moved into the new position.

During his on-the-job training, the young man attended classes and obtained certification as a wastewater treatment plant operator. He went on to earn an associate's degree in the field. Then he found a chemistry program at a nearby university and earned a bachelor's degree, all while working full-time. This young man's transformation from a high school graduate to a skilled technician and chemist occurred because opportunities for learning existed at his workplace. When asked if he had had such goals in mind when he entered the workforce, he responded, "I always wanted to go to college, but I never thought I would have the chance."

Enhanced Employment Security

Many companies today need employees who are adaptable, flexible, and open to change—in other words, people who are learning. Learning

sharpens mental skills. Learners are able to respond more effectively to a changing environment and adapt to new situations. In short, they become more valuable to the organization—their positions become more secure.

Workforce reduction is still an unfortunate component of today's business world, and it is no longer practical to plan on simply getting a job and staying with it for an entire career. In today's downsized world, companies often flatten their hierarchies. This means there are fewer opportunities for promotion. Being employed today is no guarantee of work tomorrow. Learning gives you more control over your own destiny—it makes you employable.

Employability

Being employable is of more lasting benefit than simply having a job. It means that, wherever you go, companies will want to hire you because of your skills and knowledge. Learning is portable, unlike training, which is often employer specific.

Sometimes, an awareness of employability is a liberating experience. For example, the quality manager of a paperboard company felt trapped in his job. He challenged himself to identify his skills and understand his value to the company. He realized that he was afraid of doing something wrong, and this fearfulness was causing him to feel trapped. He decided to leave the company after he completed several important projects. Due to his newfound sense of freedom, the manager was more creative and innovative. Others responded to his self-confidence with increased attention. After recognizing his skills and value—his employability—the quality manager felt free to perform wholeheartedly in his current job. He is still there.

Increased Wages

Enhanced learning may result in an increase in wages. One recent survey suggests that, on average, workers receive an 8% increase in wages for each additional year of schooling (National Center on the Educational Quality of the Workforce, 1995). Although learning is not quite the same as schooling, in that there are no credits or degrees earned, it does result in desirable qualities such as flexibility and the ability to respond to

change. There is good reason to expect learning to have a positive impact on wages because learning applied to work increases productivity and quality.

Organizations that sponsor learning in the workplace and individuals who engage in learning are not the only ones to benefit. There are advantages for those who set up the system within the organization as well.

Benefits to Human Resources Development Staff

The human resources, training, human resources development, or organization development staff responsible for creating learning opportunities are likely to realize many benefits in fulfilling organizational goals while enhancing the progress of employees.

More Bang for the Buck

Informal learning is less costly than traditional training. Employees do not necessarily have to leave their worksites, there is no tuition, and expenses for supplies are minimal or nonexistent. Therefore, costs associated with this type of learning are likely to be significantly lower.

Increased Pool of Human Capital

Staff succession is a critical issue in many organizations. Because people are developing themselves, some employees who are considered unqualified for additional growth and development can become learners and increase their capabilities. As a result, there will be an enlarged pool of human capital from which to draw when openings occur.

Adding Meaning to Your Work

Creating a system for learning means adding another dimension to the role of the development staff. They become facilitators of others' learning, which gives them the opportunity to experience the joy of helping others. When people who never thought of themselves as creative are able to solve difficult problems or complete tasks they did not believe they had the skills and knowledge to perform, being part of their success is a valuable benefit in itself.

Overcoming Barriers to Learning

So far, we've described all the benefits of creating systems for learning within organizations. There are some potential drawbacks too—from both organizational and individual perspectives. Thoroughly understanding the disadvantages may help in devising mechanisms for turning them into advantages.

Overcoming Organizational Barriers

Once they are learners, employees may become bored with their jobs. Should this occur, your investment in learning could simply walk out the door to another employer. While considering this possibility, it is important to remember two things:

- Employment is an economic exchange. When a company invests in an employee, it receives the benefit of the person's greater knowledge and skills while he or she is employed there. The economic reality is that this investment does pay a return during the time the worker is there.

- Other employers may not provide learning opportunities. As indicated earlier, learning can become addictive. If employees realize that learning is a benefit, they may choose to forgo higher wages in exchange for quality-of-life benefits such as the opportunity to learn. The challenge for the organization is to make certain the employee is aware of the value of learning.

Learning is a way of generating wealth and a competitive advantage for the sponsoring organization. In the words of one satisfied employer, "We are investing in the company's future and the future of employees. The benefit to us is a competitive advantage" (Goldberg, 1999). For individuals, learning is an opportunity to increase self-esteem and employability. The organization that provides learning as a benefit furthers itself as well as the employee.

Overcoming Individual Barriers

Individuals engaged in learning in the workplace may also encounter some uncomfortable situations, such as admission of error, failure to

reach learning goals, and challenges to previously held beliefs. However, if employees think through these three issues, they can devise ways to address the difficulties.

- An employee may have to admit an error or a previous lack of knowledge. One of the participants at a Workplace Learning Conference (contact www.cew.wisc.edu/workplace for additional information) was describing a program created specifically to assist people in obtaining their high school equivalency diploma. A man who worked at a plant had inquired about this program, but he was concerned about the application form he had filled out 31 years earlier, in which he had stated that he had a high school diploma. He did not have one, but he was convinced at the time that he would not get the job without it. Now he was afraid that he might be fired because he had been untruthful. As it turned out, he wasn't dismissed from his job for not telling the truth 31 years ago, but he underwent more than a little discomfort owning up to his falsehood. The company, realizing the value of the worker's long experience and positive record, chose to overlook the indiscretion. The employee went on to enjoy the company's learning opportunities, and both parties prospered from the experience. The drawback in this instance was having to confess to an untruth.

- A more likely situation for most people is the possibility of failing to achieve a learning goal. This fear is particularly acute for people who have been out of school for a long time or who did not do well when they were in school. If they do not realize that they have been learning throughout their lives, it can be a frightening prospect. On the other hand, even not reaching a set goal represents some forward movement because the employee has at least tried something new. This is not failure—it is a form of success.

- Another possibility is that entrenched beliefs will be challenged by new knowledge. This can be an uncomfortable situation. Challenging long-held beliefs may cause people to wonder about the value of their past experiences. Realizing that today is different from yesterday and that what was true then may not be true now can help us to understand that we were not necessarily wrong in the past. Different times require fresh attitudes and assumptions.

In Chapter 1, we discussed the characteristics of learning in organizations. In this chapter, we developed an understanding of some of the potential benefits of learning for organizations and individuals. Chapter 3 will discuss approaches to adult workplace learning and their implications for creating a system for individual learning in organizations.

3

Working with Adult Learning Styles and Practices

We teachers . . . are in the grip of an astonishing delusion. We think that we can take a picture, a structure, a working model of something, constructed in our minds out of long experience and familiarity, and by turning that model into a string of words, transplant it whole into the mind of someone else.

J. HOLT
How Children Learn

The Compact Oxford English Dictionary (Simpson and Weiner, 1991) defines the word *learn* as "to acquire knowledge of a subject or skill . . . as a result of study, experience, or teaching." Learning, then, is the act of acquiring knowledge. Traditionally, when we think of trying to learn something, we think of going to a class and being taught by someone. While this may accomplish the goal in many instances, it excludes two-thirds of the definition of learning—that of acquiring knowledge by study or experience.

Learning Is . . .

Learning is the act of acquiring new knowledge by any means. Who can judge whether someone has learned something? Often only the person doing the learning is capable of doing so. Learning may take place through silent reflection, listening and synthesizing, hands-on application, or active experimentation. Learning may be abstract, or it may be concrete.

When people consciously seek out learning opportunities, they may be considered to be in the learning mode. The learning mode concept originates in adult learning theory. There are a variety of theories about adult learning. Examining them may help us to identify how a focus on learning can augment the more traditional training and education already taking place in organizations.

Major Adult Learning Theories

Merriam and Caffarella (1999) describe five main schools of thought on adult learning: behaviorist, cognitive, humanist, social learning, and constructivist.

- The *behaviorist* looks for observable changes in behavior, not in thought processes. From this perspective, learning occurs in response to changes in the learner's environment. According to the work of B. F. Skinner (1974), the teacher's role is to ensure that learners attain learning objectives that are set by the teacher or other interested parties. The teacher also manipulates the environment so that learning can occur. Behavioral learning theorists often sequence learning activities from simple to complex. This view of learning is extremely task oriented.

- *Cognitive* theorists look at perception, insight, and meaning. For them, learning occurs when experiences are reorganized to make sense of things in the environment. Also known as Gestaltists, cognitive theorists draw on the work of Jean Piaget (1966). While the leader structures the content of the learning activity, the learner controls the learning process. The goal of learning is to develop skills and capacity.

- The *humanist* is mainly interested in the human potential for growth. In the humanist perspective, people should be involved in their own learning, which should be self-initiated and largely self-managed. The humanist believes that learning fundamentally changes the learner, who should evaluate its impact. The humanist approach is exemplified in the works of Abraham Maslow (1965), Malcolm Knowles (1980), and Carl Rogers (1983). From the hu-

manist perspective, the leader acts as a facilitator and guide, respecting the integrity and ability of the learner. Learning is seen as a democratic, cooperative process.

- The *social learning* view presumes that we learn by observing others and by the consequences of that observation. After observing, we store the information and compare it to our own approach. When the need arises, we act, using the new knowledge. Then we assess how the process went and modify behavior accordingly. Learning happens in a social context. The teacher's role is to be a model for the learner. Albert Bandura (1976) exemplifies the work of the social learning theorists.

- *Constructivists* believe that learning is a process of constructing meaning—it is how we make sense of things we experience directly or talk about with others. We learn by adapting to what we experience in our environment. Constructivists view the leader as a facilitator who negotiates learning objectives with the learner. Constructivist learning theory is derived from the work of John Dewey (1938), Thomas Kuhn (1962), and Jean Piaget (1966).

Adult Workplace Learning

The practice of adult workplace learning derives largely from the humanist and constructivist schools of learning. The humanist believes that, to a large degree, we can control our own destinies, that we are inherently good and want to do the right thing, that we are free to act, that our behavior is a consequence of choice, that we possess unlimited potential for growth and development (Maslow, 1970; Rogers, 1983)—and that, although this growth and development occurs in the individual, there is also a distinct benefit to the organization.

The constructivist believes that learning is not merely a transmission of information but a subjective process of creating knowledge that is unique to each individual: What you learn from a specific experience may be very different from what I learn from the same event. Additionally, not all knowledge can be taught by a teacher who presumably knows the answers. In other words, to some extent, learning is subjective. "Truth" to me may be different from "truth" to you.

When designing a workplace learning system, we must consider a number of issues, including the following:

- How sophisticated are the learners about learning? Are they already used to learning, or are they likely to be somewhat intimidated by it?

- What outcomes are sought from the learning experience?

- What is the learner's learning style? Does he or she learn better by experimenting or by reflecting? By listening to someone speak or by conversing with the person?

- What context is most appropriate for the learner and for the subject matter to be learned? Some topics demand a traditional classroom setting. Others are better suited to a semiformal, facilitated environment. Still others are best learned informally.

Considering each of these items contributes to a successful learning system. Learning programs often must aim for the lowest common denominator—the lowest common level of knowledge of those in the session. Learning program planners may also hold beginning or advanced sessions. With a flexible learning approach, they can tailor the learning opportunity to the particular learner. It is important to consider the stages of learning, potential outcomes of learning, learning styles, and learning contexts. We will also discuss the role of the person creating the learning opportunities.

Stages of Learning

People are often at different stages in learning the same skill or set of information. One person may be a novice and not know anything about a topic, while another is fairly well informed but needs assistance figuring out how to move beyond his or her current level of knowledge. Paul Hersey and Kenneth Blanchard (1988) suggest that there are four distinct stages of learner development.

In Stage 1, learners are unsure of their learning skills. They are just beginning to learn and are often uncertain even of how to begin. They have low levels of self-direction and are used to relying on a teacher to tell them what to do. The learner at Stage 1 is not in a learning mode and will likely need assistance to enter it. At this level, learners may even fight

against employer-sponsored learning, and they may be wary of the employer's motives. As one suspicious employee put it, "Management wouldn't really want to help employees improve, so this must just be a ploy to get us to change careers and leave the organization so that our jobs can be eliminated."

Traditional training or educational programs often make sense at Stage 1, but so do opportunities that engage developing learners in learning that is valuable to them. Initially, the learning that takes place may not even be work related. The idea is to get people started so that learning becomes fun and eventually a way of life.

Stage 2 learners may still need assistance to get into the learning mode. They are usually motivated but do not know much about the subject matter and may be only moderately self-directed in terms of pursuing a topic that interests them. Stage 2 learners frequently need someone to identify what is important for them to learn or to suggest how they might go about learning it. Trainers must adopt a more facilitative style, assisting learners in framing what they need to learn but allowing them to take more responsibility for defining the learning process.

Stage 3 learners have the skills and basic knowledge of learning. They are already in the learning mode. They see themselves as ready to explore a subject area on their own, provided they have a good guide to assist them when they need it. They may still need help in refining learning goals and identifying mechanisms for learning.

Stage 4 learners are highly self-directed. They are willing and able to plan, execute, and evaluate their own learning. While a resource person may be of assistance from time to time, Stage 4 learners will manage their own learning for the most part. A new manager who developed facilitation skills illustrates the progression through the four stages of learner development.

Randy, a young manager, had a goal of learning facilitation skills. Although he had attended meetings, he had never really thought about what it would take to be in the leadership role. After a recent promotion, he had to lead meetings in a manner that would involve all of the participants. He sought out a training session provided by an outside vendor. He was disappointed in the program, not for its content, which was quite good, but because he did not get a chance to practice any of the skills he learned. Randy was at Stage 1. He was a novice at learning about facilitation skills. The classroom format helped him identify some

concepts but did not satisfy all his requirements. He was ready to move to Stage 2.

Randy consulted with the learning resources person at his company and decided that a good way to learn was to actually apply the skills. He was somewhat intimidated by the process, so he located a person in the company who he believed had good facilitation skills. Randy sat in on several meetings led by this experienced manager. After each session, the two of them sat down and discussed what had happened, what was successful, and what could have been done better. Through this process, Randy gained confidence and developed an understanding of the facilitation process.

When he felt comfortable enough, Randy arranged for the first meeting of a group he was to facilitate. During Stage 3 of Randy's learning process, the manager who was working with him assisted in creating his agenda and even sat in on the meeting. Afterward, the two met for a debriefing. At this point, Randy felt he could create the agenda for the second meeting and lead it himself; he simply met with his mentor afterward. From then on, Randy conducted the meetings on his own.

This process allowed Randy to gradually learn the skills. While he was building confidence, he had the assistance of a manager/mentor. When he felt secure enough, he launched himself. Each individual goes through similar stages of learning most new skills. By planning out the process, learning can be much more effective.

Learning to Learn

At Stage 4, it is ideal for the learner to "learn to learn," so that any activity can become a learning one. How do people move to this level? One way is by becoming aware of themselves, their learning process, and the opportunities for learning that surround them every day. Past exposure to independent learning makes it easier to progress to this level. Many learners may never master the skill of learning to learn.

Peter Vaill (1998) believes the best approach is to adopt learning as a way of being. Learning as a way of being has seven components: self-directed learning, creative learning, expressive learning, feeling learning, online learning, continuous learning, and reflexive learning.

1. *Self-directed learners* are the only ones who know their particular learning needs; they must be responsible for determining these needs

and making them known. While they may have assistance in locating resources, they are responsible for the learning—no one will provide it for them if they don't take a proactive stance.

2. In *creative learning*, there are no preset goals or predetermined methods for learning. Creative learners explore without knowing exactly where they are going, yet they are aware that learning is taking place.

3. *Expressive learning* comes from opportunities that emerge in daily life. They are not planned or created but occur in the course of one's daily experiences.

4. *Feeling learners* know what they are learning at a deep and personal level. This requires reflection on what they have realized.

5. *Online learning* refers to learning while working. It is, perhaps, the most common way for working people to learn, because the workplace provides them with new opportunities on a fairly regular basis.

6. *Continuous learners* regard learning as a lifelong endeavor. They choose to learn from every situation.

7. *Reflexive learners* learn about their own learning processes. In learning how to learn, they generate the knowledge and skill to act effectively in any learning situation.

Learning to learn is about consciously choosing to learn from an experience and taking the time to reflect on it to determine what has been learned.

Abilities Needed for Learning to Learn

Learning to learn is the ability to find, analyze, capture, store, and retrieve knowledge and information. Effective learners know where to begin looking for information. We do not always learn in the same way. For instance, for most subjects, a primary learning style may involve reading, then experimenting with new ideas, then reading and experimenting some more. Learners who utilize this style may only be comfortable conversing about the subject and gaining additional insight from other people's perspectives when they are fairly knowledgeable about at least the basics of a topic. They may reverse experimentation and

reading when they are learning about a technical subject, such as a new computer program. After learners have experimented, they may go to the manual to explore some of the program's intricacies. Again, when some level of proficiency is achieved, these learners can talk to others about it or understand discussions about how to use the program more effectively or efficiently. Other types of learners may thrive on talking to others about the program before they know a thing about it. They learn from the conversation and then apply what they have learned. Awareness of these nuances assists in learning to learn.

Outcomes of Learning

Merriam and Caffarella (1999) identify the following four potential outcomes of learning:

1. *Cognitive or knowledge learning* develops understanding. Learners may not be able to do something differently, but they comprehend it in a new way. If production employees spend a day observing a salesperson's work, they may not know how to sell, but they will have gained a broader understanding of certain aspects of the job.

2. *Attitude and values learning* results in a change in perception. Something that was previously important is no longer significant. It may be replaced by a new value. Entering a learning mode is an example of a changed attitude for someone who previously discounted learning because "it only happens in schools."

3. *Skill development,* which may be physical, mental, or social, leads to an ability to do something that was not possible before. This is perhaps the most common form of workplace learning because people usually need to learn new skills in a new job.

4. *Aspiration learning* changes a person's goals. The young man who began his career in production and became a wastewater treatment plant operator with a degree in chemistry is an example of someone whose aspirations changed. He began with a vague desire to go on to school and acquired an education that made him a scientist.

   Each of these outcomes is valuable in different situations. In designing a learning system, we must consider the outcomes provided by each component of the system in order to create a holistic program.

Learning Style: How Adults Learn

Ornstein (1977) attributes learning to different forms of consciousness: the left brain and the right brain. The left brain is analytical and logical, whereas the right brain is visual, intuitive, creative, and imaginative. He suggests that people whose left brains are dominant acquire different kinds of knowledge, and in different ways, than do those whose right brains are dominant. Similarly, Hudson (1986) distinguishes between divergent and convergent thinking. The divergent thinker is imaginative, whereas the convergent thinker is logical and analytical. Other writers further differentiate learning approaches.

Learning Styles

Kolb (1984) views learning as a circular process directly related to experience. For each person, knowledge is created through an experience. The individual learning process depends on personal style. We attain knowledge through concrete experience, through reflective observation, through abstract concepts, or through experimenting with alternatives.

Honey and Mumford (1986) identified four basic learning styles that coincide with Kolb's styles: the activist, who is open-minded and enthusiastic; the pragmatist, who is a down-to-earth problem solver; the theorist, who is logical and analytical; and the reflector, who is cautious and observant. To be most effective, learning systems should be designed with opportunities that accommodate each of these styles.

Tendency Toward Preferences

In designing systems with learning preferences in mind, it is important to realize that we instinctively favor our own learning style. Without realizing it, many of us tend to set up learning situations for others based on our primary learning styles—not theirs. From an organizational perspective, understanding of different styles will help you reframe your perceptions of learning so that you can design learning opportunities for a variety of styles. From an individual perspective, an awareness of personal learning styles will help you differentiate between learning situations that require catering to your own style and learning opportunities that require a design for a different learning style.

Thus far, we have discussed learning as it is occurring. Learning contexts may vary.

Contexts for Learning

Learning takes place in different locations. The most common site for learning is based on the institutional model, exemplified by our public education system. The institutional model has three main goals (Vaill, 1998): First, the learner expects an instructor to teach what needs to be known. Second, it is assumed that the learner values the goal—in other words, it is a moral duty to go to school and learn. Third, the learner does not determine the goals—more knowledgeable individuals, such as teachers or school boards, determine what is to be learned.

The key to learning in the institutional model is to learn efficiently, as quickly as possible, and to cover as much material as possible in the allocated time period. Institutionalized learning is answer oriented. The content is already known. As children, we come to understand that learning takes place in schools. As we mature into adults, this presumption is often carried with us. On the basis of our experience, we assume that learning takes place in a formal setting. Organizations have often adopted the institutional model and fostered formal learning settings. The reality for adults in the workplace is that the formal setting is only one of several learning contexts.

Formal Learning

Formal learning takes place in a classroom. Generally, the instructor already knows what is to be learned and has created mechanisms by which to transfer knowledge or skill to learners. This form of education often results in a degree or continuing education credits of some sort. Skills such as social interaction and learning to learn are not generally taught in formal education programs.

Semiformal Learning

In semiformal learning, the room is often arranged in conference style rather than classroom style, so that participants can talk to one another. The facilitator provides a broad outline of the general content as well as some specific content, but there are no predetermined answers. Rather than teaching a preset curriculum, the facilitator draws from the participants' ideas and experiences. The responsibility for learning rests with the learners.

Team training is an example of semiformal learning. Operating under the assumption that the way you get teamwork is to give the team work, an effective approach to teaching teamwork is to turn the class into a team and give them some work to do. As they perform their tasks, issues arise and are addressed situationally, in the context of teamwork. Some of the learning is about becoming a member of a team—a part of a community.

Nonformal Learning

Nonformal learning occurs in various places. It is often planned but generally takes place in a nonclassroom setting. While there may be a facilitator or group leader, learners are largely responsible for their own learning. For instance, the Metropolitan Milwaukee Association of Commerce sponsors a series of learning circles. These groups of five to eight people meet monthly to discuss chapters in a nonfiction, business-related book. The experience is quite different from going to a class or seminar—the learners direct the content and the process. Nonformal learning may also take place in churches, on nonprofit boards, and in other voluntary associations.

Informal Learning

Informal learning is acquired from life experiences. It is the independent pursuit of learning. Watkins and Marsick (1993) characterize informal learning as the ability to systematically reflect on an experience and view it as an opportunity for learning. It includes the capacity to apply what has been learned to later experiences and a personally motivated desire to learn.

Another type of informal learning is the incidental, or unplanned, variety. Learning that takes place spontaneously is incidental (Lankard, 1995). Skills, knowledge, or understanding improve in the process of doing something. Incidental learning may also take place through making mistakes or by being part of informal networks. Incidental learning becomes effective when the learner reflects on it.

At least four categories of work-related skills may be learned informally: cultural, intrapersonal, interpersonal, and job specific/technical (Grolnic, 1999). The latter is generally learned most effectively through a formal training program, but it may also be learned informally

TABLE 1   CONTINUUM OF LEARNING CONTEXTS

HIGH STRUCTURE			LOW STRUCTURE
←			→
FORMAL	SEMIFORMAL	NONFORMAL	INFORMAL

- *Formal:* Inside formal, established system. Led by expert.
- *Semiformal:* Organized inside formal, established system. Facilitated, not directed.
- *Nonformal:* Organized, but outside formal, established system. May be facilitated, may be self-directed.
- *Informal:* Outside or inside formal organization. Self-directed.

through on-the-job training. Although the other three concepts may be taught in a formally presented workshop, they are best learned informally. Skill building and behavioral change happen through practice, which generally occurs informally.

Many of the concepts we have explored blend together to create a workplace learning environment. Table 1 depicts the range of informal to formal learning environments. The continuum can become blurred, for instance, when informal learning takes place in formal settings as learners reflect on how new understandings relate to their previous knowledge. No learning environment is better than another. It is important to remember that different types of learning will occur in different environments. Later chapters will discuss designing learning systems that are applicable to each setting because individuals may tend to favor one environment over another and different formats may be more appropriate for certain types of learning opportunities.

Lessons for the Learning Facilitator

The learning facilitator's method of framing learning opportunities has a major impact on the learning outcome. In individual learning, the leader's role is facilitative—to assist learners in devising and following their own learning programs. Leaders place minimal restrictions on learners. Learners are allowed to choose approaches that are most convenient and/or appropriate. Leaders assist learners in overcoming blocks to learning and learners select how they will demonstrate what they have learned, but the leader may assist them in understanding their options by providing a range of resources. Depending on how much progress learners have made in learning to learn, leaders assist in defining goals, locating resources, and clarifying understandings. This may be done one-on-one or in small groups.

Leaders may need to help learners identify their learning needs and interests because learners are often unclear about specifics. Leaders may also identify and facilitate the use of community learning resources.

The responsibility of the trainer/facilitator changes as the learner develops. At Stage 1, the trainer has responsibility for the content and process of learning. In Stages 2, 3, and 4, increasing amounts of responsibility are transferred to learners. At first, the facilitator may need to actively engage learners in their own learning. By Stage 4, learners will assertively take responsibility. Facilitators need to be flexible with learning approaches in order to accommodate the needs of learners who are moving through the different stages of learning.

In summary, before learning in the workplace can be effective, learners must develop the skills of questioning, listening, and reflecting. They must process newly obtained information or acquire the knowledge and skills to learn effectively in a variety of situations. The role of the learning resources staff is to facilitate this transition.

Summary

A partial goal of creating workplace learning opportunities is to move toward Vaill's concept of learning as a way of being. If your organization is filled with people who consciously practice these skills, the company will be better able to respond to changes—both environmental and self-imposed. When such skills are prevalent, problems tend to be viewed as learning opportunities.

 Learning to learn means being able to create mechanisms for learning when such mechanisms are not directly accessible or even visible. It is about going beyond the apparent to gain additional insights. How does this concept translate into learning in the workplace? Step-by-step. This cannot be accomplished overnight. You must create opportunities to get people in a learning mode and actively seeking more "created" forms of learning. Then you may introduce concepts of learning to learn.

Eventually people will begin to take responsibility for their own learning and will search for ways to learn in almost any situation.

As you establish a learning system, the following key components need to be considered:

• What stage of learning is targeted?

• What context is appropriate for the learning opportunity?

• Which learning styles are most easily accommodated?

• What outcome do you seek? A change in knowledge, attitude or values, skill level, or aspiration?

• Is there a way to redesign the opportunity to make it more applicable to the potential learners?

The concepts of learning stages, contexts, styles, and outcomes serve as reference points for the discussion of the learning programs and processes in Part 3. They are also used as tools for selecting your organization's overall learning system in Part 2.

P A R T   2

CREATING A SYSTEM
TO SUPPORT LEARNING

Tell me, I will forget. Show me, I may remember. But involve me and I will understand.

CHINESE PROVERB

The previous chapters gave an overview of adult learning in organizations and related the concepts to practical experience. Part 2 will focus on creating a learning system. While it is possible to simply pick out a few approaches from Part 3, learning will have a greater impact if you implement a program systematically. Depending on your organization's needs, you may want to start small and build a system over time, or you may prefer to create a full-blown system immediately. Either way, it will be helpful to think through what a learning system might look like.

Learning in organizations will be difficult, if not impossible, to sustain without organizational support. One form of support is the purposeful establishment of learning opportunities. Another is to link learning with organizational systems.

Part 2 describes a <u>five-phase strategy for the design and implementation of a learning system</u>. The phases consist of

1. Exploration

2. Envisioning

√3. Planning

√4. Incubation and development

√5. Implementation and improvement

Chapter 4 contains an overview of the five phases and a detailed description of Phases 1, 2, and 3. It also covers many principles that may underlie an organizational learning system, which you may draw on as you prepare your own system. These standards are not all-encompassing, nor are they all applicable to every organization; but they provide a beginning point from which to develop a mission for your learning system. They can help you evaluate what you want your system to accomplish and which components you believe are critical for your organization. It is important to align your learning system with your organization's culture and history. Chapter 4 provides a mechanism to assist you in selecting appropriate enhancements for individual learning in your organization.

Chapter 5 covers Phases 4 and 5 and addresses support systems that will sustain your learning system over time. Many organizations have started learning efforts; not all of them succeed, often because built-in, organizational support mechanisms are missing. This chapter discusses a variety of important support systems that will help you achieve the level of endorsement necessary to sustain a learning system.

4

Developing a Vision, Mission, and Plan

What we have created so far is not good enough. Existing systems of education and training tend to favor an elite of fast learners. . . . If we are to reach the unreached and include the excluded, more must mean different.

D. STEWART AND C. BALL
Lifelong Learning, Developing Human Potential

The strategy for designing and implementing a learning system consists of five phases:

1. *Exploration:* Includes designating the learning system planning chair and creating a planning team. Initiate the process by determining who will work on creating the system and defining the extent of their authority.

2. *Envisioning:* Includes determining the relevance of learning to the organizational mission, identifying the underlying principles of the system, and developing a mission for it.

3. *Planning:* Encompasses analyzing the facility and current learning opportunities, planning the learning system components, determining staffing needs, and budgeting.

4. *Incubation and development:* Includes developing learning opportunities and a learning space, planning and implementing marketing strategy, and developing an organizational support system.

5. *Implementation and improvement:* Comprises a kickoff event and evaluation of and improvement to the program content.

TABLE 2   CREATION STRATEGY FOR THE LEARNING FUNCTION

PHASE 1: EXPLORATION

- Determine to create a learning system
- Designate planning chair
- Create planning team

PHASE 2: ENVISIONING

- Identify relationship to organizational mission
- Select underlying principles
- Create learning unit mission

PHASE 3: PLANNING

- Analyze current learning opportunities
- Plan components
- Conduct facility analysis
- Determine staffing needs
- Create a budget

PHASE 4: INCUBATION AND DEVELOPMENT

- Develop opportunities
- Develop learning space
- Plan and implement marketing strategy
- Develop support system

PHASE 5: IMPLEMENTATION AND IMPROVEMENT

- Kickoff event
- Evaluate content of programming

This chapter focuses on the first three phases—exploration, envisioning, and planning. All five phases of this strategy are detailed in Table 2.

Phase 1: Exploration

In Phase 1, you determine to create a learning system. Although it may be too early to decide who will staff the program, a planning team and team leader should be selected. The leader should have strong facilitation, planning, and project management skills. The team may be made up entirely of human resources or training staff; however, other staff members can provide valuable input and assistance when it comes time to market and implement the system throughout the organization. Additional members of the team could come from various units. Ideally, every major functional unit should be represented, but it is wise to keep the group to less than 10 people.

From the beginning, this team should understand the following process-related parameters:

- Is there a commitment to move ahead with a learning system, or is this just an exploratory team?

- Is the committee for planning purposes only, or does it have the authority to implement as well?

- Is there a preset budget? Is the team supposed to create it? If so, who will approve it, and what is the approval process?

- If the planning team determines staffing is necessary, will money be available?

Once the team is formed, you may need to conduct some exploration to ensure that each member understands the team's purpose and goals. You may want to share this book with the members or summarize it in written form or by some other means of presentation. The team may also want to visit organizations that have already created learning systems. Afterwards, the team should create a vision of a learning system appropriate for your organization.

Phase 2: Envisioning

In Phase 2, the team will envision your learning system. As shown in Table 2, this phase includes identifying the relationship of learning to the organizational mission, selecting the underlying principles for your learning system, and creating your learning unit mission.

Identifying Relationship to Organizational Mission

Your learning system must relate somehow to the overall mission of the organization. This does not mean that the organizational mission statement has to be revised. Learning is often already implicitly included in statements that refer to individual performance, continuous improvement, or customer service, all of which require people who are learning. This should be highlighted in your learning unit's mission statement. To create your statement, articulate the tenets that best describe your organization's commitment to learning; then base your mission on those principles.

Learning Principles in Organizations

While each organization is unique, you should have some basic understanding of your organization's beliefs about learning. The following list of organization-related principles may be helpful in designing a mission or philosophy statement for your learning system:

- Continuous lifelong learning must become a standard feature of the workplace. Organizations in which there is little or no learning won't be competitive in tomorrow's business environment.

- When possible, learning must be taken out of the classroom and placed in the context of the situation under consideration.

- Increased learning will facilitate better responses to a continually changing world.

- The organization must encourage and enable learning.

- Many people are averse to learning because of bad experiences in traditional schools. To overcome this resistance, inviting learning opportunities can be created that will lead to more focused, work-related learning.

- Everyone should have easy access to learning opportunities, which, as much as possible, should not be restrictive as to time or place.

- Learners should have access to guidance and collaborative support.

- All learning—formal, semiformal, nonformal, and informal—has value.

- Employees and management must both be involved in developing, designing, and implementing learning opportunities.

- Technology and other learning aids may be incorporated, but not to the exclusion of other methods.

You may also wish to incorporate some of the following individual-related principles in designing a mission for your learning system:

- Learners must be responsible for learning. The ultimate goal is self-directed learning, in which individuals "own" their learning and learning processes.

- Whenever possible, learners should initiate the learning process to meet their needs.

- Learning opportunities must be relevant to each persons' needs and interests.

- People should become conscious, intentional, and reflective about their learning.

- Sometimes, learning involves unlearning present beliefs and ideas.

- Learning should build on what people already know—even unlearning builds on a base.

- Traditional training has a place in skill development, but does not help people move beyond the training. Only learning, and learning to learn, improves our ability to adapt to change.

- People have different learning styles. It is important for each person to understand his or her individual style and match that style to a learning method.

- Everyone can learn.

- Each employee (salaried and hourly, exempt and nonexempt) should have a development plan. This plan should be a living document that is updated regularly. Developing and fulfilling the plan is the employee's responsibility; however, assistance should be provided on request.

- Learning should relate to the work being done.

This is a broad array of statements about learning. Some of them will be applicable to your organization, others may not be. Which ones best fit your organization's culture? Which absolutely do not fit? Choose a maximum of five concepts that you believe are critical to your organization. How would you state them? List the five principles that best fit your organization's culture and learning needs.

Learning Unit Mission

"Provide opportunities for individual development through facilitating learning and education in a positive environment" is the learning system mission statement of Cominco (DeBiasio et al., 1999). Gehl Company's mission for its learning center is "to provide the opportunity to improve work relationships and interpersonal skills for employees as well as to encourage self-confidence and a positive attitude," because "learning is forever" (Harlaquinn et al., 1999).

Once you have defined the relationship between learning and the organization's mission and identified the relevant principles, the next step is to articulate the mission of the learning system. What goals have you set for your learning system? You may want to ensure that some form of learning is available for individual, peer-based, and group needs. You may want programs to get people into a learning mode and to provide opportunities for ongoing learning and learning to learn.

You might also consider additional questions. Will you integrate your learning system with your training system or with career development? Will it be a separate, stand-alone function or will it be housed within another area? Your answers are critical; they will help you select learning opportunities for your system as you move into Phase 3.

Follow up a short mission statement with an in-depth description of the organization's underlying philosophy of learning, which would likely contain statements about why it is important. Include references to organizational and individual learning. Using the five principles you identified earlier concerning your organization's beliefs about learning, write a short mission statement followed by a narrative that includes the learning principles.

You have now envisioned a learning system. How would you depict this system if you were describing it to others? Figures 1 and 2 illustrate different learning systems. Figure 1 displays the learning unit as a puzzle. The system itself is held together by four major components: individual learning, peer-based learning, group learning, and support systems. Figure 2 is more like a traditional organizational chart except that it focuses on the components of a learning system. There probably would not be a person to coordinate each component—the chart is just a way to visualize a system.

Which figure looks more like the system you are creating? What labels would you use? Would you create an entirely different diagrammatic view? If so, what would it be?

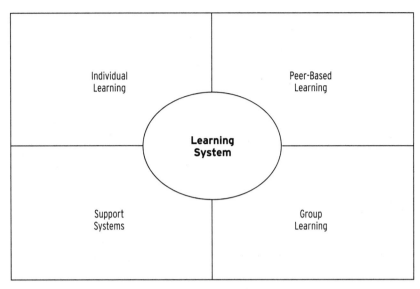

Figure 1   Diagrammatic View of Learning Function

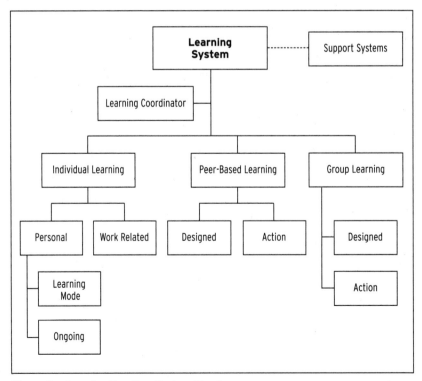

Figure 2   Learning Function System Chart

Naming Your Learning System

Finally, what will you call your learning system? Some organizations prefer a plain-vanilla title like "Learning System." Others are more creative. Some options include

- Roads Scholar Program

- Member Development

- Personal Development

- REAL: Refresh Education And Learning (DeBiasio et al., 1999)

- PETE: Personal Enrichment Through Education

Now that you have envisioned and named your system, the next step is to plan the specific components.

Phase 3: Planning

Phase 3 consists of analyzing the learning activities and spaces that are currently available in your organization, deciding what new opportunities to offer, determining the need for staff, and calculating the first year's budget. Planning an entire system is a complicated endeavor. Each piece is presented here in a linear fashion due to the structure imposed by the writing process. The creation of your plan may be more chaotic. You will probably move from one topic to another and back again. This nonlinear approach will help you develop a richer, more complete learning system.

Analysis of Current Learning

Prior to planning your entire system, it will be helpful to analyze the current learning opportunities in your organization. You may do this by conducting an informal organizational survey, talking to people in each department to determine what they do to learn. Use Exercise 1 to record each activity. You may find it useful to review the exercise briefly before beginning.

Before you select the new components of your learning system, you will need to decide where the process will occur, especially when it takes place away from the work site.

EXERCISE 1: LEARNING OPPORTUNITY SELECTION GRID

To the best of your ability, identify the stage of the learner involved in each activity, the context, the learning style accommodated, and the outcome of the learning. Indicate your assessments in the appropriate boxes.

| Offering | Type of Learning | | | Stage of Learner | | | Context | | | | Learning Style Accommodated | | | | Outcome of Learning | | | |
	Individual	Peer	Group	1	2	3	4	F	S	N	I	A	P	T	R	Knowledge	Attitude/Values	Skill	Aspiration

F = Formal, S = Semiformal, N = Nonformal, I = Informal, A = Activist, P = Pragmatist, T = Theorist, R = Reflector

Analysis of Learning Space

Nonformal and informal learning may occur anywhere in an organization while work is going on. However, some nonformal learning requires a different location, as do almost all semiformal and formal learning. In a small organization, a conference center may be adequate. Does your company have space available for learning? Is it appropriate for the needs of formal, semiformal, nonformal, and informal learning? If not, what is missing? Ideally, what would you want to have? You may have space already available that can be modified to fit your needs. Some teams have found that the available space did not fit their vision for their learning space. They determined that a more functional and perhaps better learning environment could be created in a stand-alone learning center.

Johnsonville Sausage recently went through this exercise. One of the things it wanted was to provide a nonthreatening, accessible facility for learning. The company has two plants located within a mile of each other. There has been a history of mild rivalry between the two locations. In the past, the resource center was located at one plant. The employees at the other plant felt slighted, so another resource center was constructed there. Staffing became an issue; then, accessibility. The company searched for other space and found nothing that met its needs. However, it did not want to invest in constructing a new site without knowing that it would be fully utilized.

Johnsonville Sausage finally resolved the issue by creating a stand-alone facility, a double-wide trailer located at a site convenient for both plants. The Member Development Center is accessible at any hour; an employee swipe card unlocks the door and registers the participant.

The layout of the center is shown in Figure 3. The structure accommodates a flexible learning space, a library, a networked computer area with five workstations, and a private office space for the member development coordinator. The coffee station has a sink, a water cooler, a refrigerator, and cupboard space.

Taco, Inc., of Cranston, Rhode Island, constructed a 2,000-square-foot facility in 1992. It is described as "a place for employees to mingle and acquire skills other than blueprint reading or machine operating" (Taco, Inc., 1999). The goal of the company's learning systems is three-fold: First, "train all people to do their jobs better and learn higher-level jobs; second, expose them to a better quality of life; and third, have them

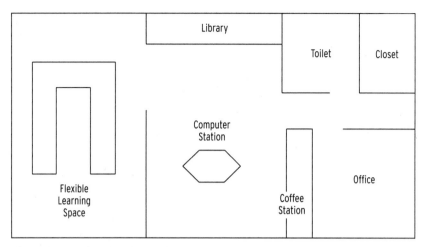

Figure 3   Member Development Center Layout

learn about government and citizenship responsibilities so they can participate" (Taco, Inc., 1999). The facility includes two classrooms, a computer lab, a library, and a conference room.

Pacific Gas & Electric's learning center is part of a conference center and hotel (Flynn, 1999). There are several meeting rooms and a 100-person auditorium complete with sound system and projection screen. The walls are covered with sound-buffered fabric that permits the hanging of flip-chart papers. Guest rooms for overnight stays are equipped with computers. There is a workout room, a movie theater, pool tables, video games, and a basketball court. The center is rented out to local colleges and other businesses when not in use by Pacific Gas & Electric.

Cominco's learning center has a library, a large and a small classroom, a lounge for quiet studying, a media center, and a computer laboratory (DeBiasio et al., 1999). Bostrom Seating turned an old storage room into a learning center. The Pepto-Bismol® room, as they call it, is painted pink—they think of it as soothing (Millner et al., 1999).

In 1995, with the help of a federal grant intended to upgrade the basic skills of employees, Gehl Corporation partnered with its union to create a learning center (Harlaquinn et al., 1999). They began the program by focusing on reading, math, and study skills but have expanded it to include technical skill development, computer instruction, and employee involvement. Specially trained peer advisers provide low-cost workshops and encourage fellow employees to get involved. When new learners come to the center, a resource specialist conducts a one-hour learning assessment. Each learner then establishes a learning plan. As the relationship develops, the resource specialist helps the learner identify additional learning opportunities.

The learning center has multiple purposes:

- To reinforce a culture of learning

- To enhance awareness of learning

- To provide a base for learning processes, resources, and support

- To hold formal and nonformal learning-related activities

- To provide a site for confidential one-on-one personal development planning

- To house a resource library

Potential Learning Site Components

- *Library:* Taco, Inc., has a lending library in their learning center. It stocks fiction and nonfiction books as well as cassettes and video-tapes. It also serves as an in-house research center and has become an electronic branch of a local university.

- *Computer lab:* Johnsonville Sausage has a computer lab with five networked computers in its member development center. Each has access to the Internet and is loaded with tutorial programs in the software used throughout the company. Cominco's learning center has an 11-station computer laboratory as well as a technical support person on call (DeBiasio et al., 1999).

- *Collaboration rooms:* These areas, also known as innovation centers or creativity labs, are designed to encourage new ideas and learning (Wycoff and Snead, 1999), unlike traditional meeting rooms or class-rooms, which are more suited to presentations than learning. The walls of a collaboration room may be covered with floor-to-ceiling white paperboard; markers, portable easels, flip charts, and adhesive notepads in a variety of colors are frequently found throughout the room so that new ideas can be captured visually. Tables and chairs, if any, tend to be smaller than usual and can be rearranged easily as desired. Other tools for the collaboration room might include a telephone (for outgoing calls only because incoming calls might disrupt the learning process), at least one computer with an Internet connection, a mind-mapping program such as Inspiration®, and project management software. A printer, an overhead projector with plenty of blank transparencies and markers, and a VCR may also come in handy.

- *Corporate university:* Many companies have developed a "corporate university" affiliated with a local educational institution to offer on-site degree-granting programs. Some also allow spouses and children of employees, and sometimes community members, to make use of these services as well. Corporate universities often do not offer degree programs—learning takes place but degrees are not given.

Once you have determined the nature of your learning space, you can move on to the remaining components of your system.

Determining New Offerings: Choosing Which Components to Implement

What components do you want in your learning system? In some ways, this book is like a cookbook. A cook seldom uses every recipe in a book and never all at the same time. Part 3 lists learning opportunities that focus on getting people into a learning mode, establishing ongoing individual learning, learning in one-on-one relationships, learning in groups, and integrating learning into work. Do you want or need any of these in your learning system? If not, what will your learning system offer?

Organizational Capacity

The size or type of your organization may have some impact on your decision. For instance, larger companies are more likely to try to accommodate everyone by offering all types of learning. And, if your company is small, you may not be able to afford such complexity. From another perspective, a homogeneous organization that exclusively employs accountants may need fewer types of learning, whereas an organization that employs people in many occupations requires more diversity. What additional learning elements do you need to achieve the goals described in your mission statement?

Full-blown systems are not a necessity—now or ever. You may opt to concentrate on one or two learning opportunities at a time. Experiment with them; then add them to your system if they work well. The key is to maintain some degree of flexibility, while considering the organizational resources available and the capacity of the system. The system can start piecemeal and evolve over time after successful initial efforts create demand for more learning opportunities.

The biggest obstacles to getting people involved are negative attitudes fostered by unfortunate learning experiences in childhood or early adulthood. Part of the challenge of creating a learning culture is to reduce those fears, perhaps by allowing the workplace to function as a learning environment. This may mean including learning that is not work-related in your system.

Determining Staffing Needs

Learning system staff play a critical role in establishing, supporting, and improving learning in organizations. Most companies that have successfully sustained learning created a staff position that is wholly focused on learning. People who focus some of their time on learning and the rest on other functions invariably end up spending more time on the non-learning components of their jobs. It is just too easy to say, "This is important and must be done now. The learning can always get done later."

Marquardt (1999) describes the role of the learning facilitator as a combination of coordinator, catalyst, observer, climate setter, communications enabler, and learning coach. This staff member is the champion of learning, assisting individuals or groups in locating resources and determining the appropriate learning strategies. The facilitator's role is to put the methods for learning into the hands of the learner.

Cunningham, Bennett, and Dawes (2000) identified four aspects of the facilitator role: actualization, design, management, and interaction.

1. *Actualization:* Most individuals are not familiar with concepts and models of learning. The staff person can help develop an understanding of the practical aspects of learning theory.

2. *Design:* It takes skill to create learning programs and opportunities, which differ from training programs. The facilitator must create learning opportunities, often from scratch, as there are few references on how to do it.

3. *Management:* The facilitator must also be responsible for marketing and selling learning opportunities within the organization because active learning is often a new concept. Someone must also administer details, such as arranging venues and providing materials.

4. *Interaction:* The facilitator may arrange face-to-face sessions, one-on-one or in groups, as well as create online learning communities, educational programming, and/or videoconferencing.

The relationship between the learning facilitator and the learner develops over time. In the initial phase, the learner and facilitator each get to know the other's styles and interests. Mutual trust grows as they work together and demonstrate reliability and support. In the next phase, mutual risk taking occurs as the facilitator encourages and the learner risks stretching. This is when true learning facilitation is achieved. As learners continue this process, they begin to internalize the techniques of learning to learn. Finally, the relationship changes, with the learners in the lead role and the facilitator in a less dominant position—as learners begin to take responsibility for their own learning.

To accomplish all of these tasks, the learning staff must have specific skills.

Learning Staff Skills

Self-knowledge is critical before learners are able to understand their own learning. One of the learning staff's major tasks is to facilitate self-knowledge.

✳ Learning staff people should have the following valuable skills and characteristics:

- Knowledge of how to learn so they can be good role models

- Desire to see others learn

- Supportive style

- Ability to provide feedback

- High degree of professional ethics and commitment to maintaining confidentiality

- Patience

- Listening skills—the ability to remain silent and listen to others, to paraphrase accurately what another person has said, and to hear what is not being said, or to read between the lines

- Knowledge of adult learning in theory and in practice

- Ability to discern appropriate learning media for different situations, needs, and learning styles

- Ability to challenge and confront when necessary

- Exceptional skill with asking questions, especially critical questions, when necessary

- Understanding of group process and facilitation skills

- Tolerence for ambiguity

- Ability to envision a future and creatively translate that vision into action

- Planning skills

- Reflecting skills and the ability to recall what has been done or said, to analyze and examine through dialogue and questioning, and to make sense of an event alone and with others

- Ability to handle continuous change

- Good networking skills—with individuals and groups, both inside and outside the organization

Once the learning system is established, it will probably need further development and updating. The resource person must be able to adapt and create inventive strategies to refresh the system. He or she must also promote and administer learning programs and a learning center and serve as a liaison to other units within the organization and to outside learning organizations.

This person must be visible and approachable. At Gehl Corporation, the learning staff person regularly visits the production area wearing a hard hat that identifies her as "Coordinator of Learning."

Given the history of training and learning in organizations, finding this person may not be an easy task. The skills and mentality of a first-rate facilitator of learning may be quite distinct from those of a traditional trainer or training manager. One organization spent more than six months trying to recruit a learning coordinator, only to end up developing another candidate internally. Alternatively, you might hire a person with an inclination to do the work who has already developed some of the necessary skills. In both cases, a personal coach who is skilled in this area should assist the potential resource person with attaining all of the necessary skills.

Potential Titles

What do you call your learning staff people? Traditional titles evoke specific images, so simply using something like "training director" will probably send the wrong message. Some suggestions for alternatives include

- Personal Development Coordinator

- Knowledge Officer (Brand, 1998)

- Education Development Counselors

- Employee Zealot (McCain and Pantazis, 1997) or Employee Development Zealot

- Jumpstarter (McCain and Pantazis, 1997)

- Learning Manager

- Architect of Learning (Galagan, 1994)

Depending on the size of the organization, the learning staff might consist of more than one person. For instance, one person might design the learning opportunities and market the program while another focuses specifically on one-on-one development.

Learning Champions

Ancillary to the learning staff, you may also want a person in each department who will be an advocate for learning. In addition to managers or professionals to whom employees report, learning champions work with individuals in their sections of a company. They present ideas for learning, gather input about the types of learning opportunities people would like to see, and share these data with the learning staff. In a union organization, a management and a union learning champion might work as a team in each section.

When all these components are in place, it is time to complete the budgeting process.

Budgeting

Budgeting may have been part of the development process up to this point. It may even have been a constraint placed on learning system developers by management. After the entire system has been developed, the budget should be revisited. What will all of this cost? There are many items to take into consideration.

- What will it cost to staff your learning system? Depending on the scope of the position, the salary could range from that of a training director at the high end to the equivalent of a trainer at the low end. If you choose to use learning champions in organizational units, will you charge the time they dedicate to learning to the unit itself or to the learning system account?

- What costs will be involved in creating a learning space? What furniture and equipment will be needed to make the space functional? How much will be allocated for the purchase of books, tapes, and other library resources?

- Will you need to purchase assessment instruments for personal development planning?

- Who will pay for time spent on learning activities? Possible options include (1) paying for all the time spent in learning activities; (2) paying for time spent on work-related learning activities, either for today's job or for tomorrow's, but learning for personal interest takes place on the employee's own time; and (3) paying for time spent on learning for the current job, but learning for future positions or personal interest occurs on the employee's time. There are many other viable options, but it is important to make a decision and adhere to it. What kind of approach best fits the learning principles and mission of your organization?

Remember, you do not have to create the entire system all at once. Try one of the components mentioned here and then experiment with some of the learning opportunities identified in Part 3—or create some of your own. Then grow the system over time.

The three phases enumerated in this chapter have set the stage for your learning system. In the next chapter, Phase 4 focuses on launching the system, and Phase 5 examines implementing and improving it.

Implementing and Managing a Learning Support System

There is a natural tendency for people to learn, and that learning will flourish if nourishing, encouraging environments are provided.

K. P. CROSS
Adults as Learners

The last two phases of the creation strategy for the learning system focus on bringing the system to fruition. As shown in Table 2 in Chapter 4, Phase 4 is the incubation and development stage. In this phase, you will develop and test the opportunities identified in the earlier planning phase, create the learning space and learning support systems, and design and implement a marketing strategy.

In Phase 5, a kickoff event marks the inauguration of the learning system. A lot of careful thought and hard work have gone into the process up to this point, but the job is not complete. A learning system is a work in progress. As the components of the system are implemented, they need to be continually evaluated and perhaps upgraded or replaced with creative new ideas. Before addressing implementation and improvement, a thorough examination of the incubation and development phase is necessary.

As in the previous section, a flexible approach is key. How you develop and introduce a system depends on the organizational capacity and resources available to you. Let the process evolve based on your needs.

Phase 4: Incubation and Development

In Phase 4, all of the previous work comes together. Many steps in this phase need to be accomplished concurrently. Therefore, you may wish to divide your learning system planning team into subcommittees responsible for each of the components.

Developing Opportunities

All of the learning opportunities suggested in this book were created and used by organizations to meet unique needs. To do the most good in your organization, you must develop each opportunity to fit the specific needs of your culture and of the people who will be participating in your learning system. This may require experimentation and creativity.

As a learning opportunity is developed, it should receive a trial run. The team that helped design the learning system can now help design the learning opportunities, but team members can also test the programs as they are developed. The pilot group could be expanded to include others in the organization as a way of getting them into the learning mode. They will also be helpful in marketing the program when you reach that step.

During the pilot, address questions on how the program works, what might be done to improve it, and which components should be replaced. Evaluate the learning opportunity based on its contribution to learning; then continue to develop it, modify it, or abandon it altogether.

Scheduling

Organizations generally schedule learning opportunities by determining a time they believe fits the potential participants' needs. Cominco's philosophy is that if learners can take the time to learn, the learning staff can be sure to schedule opportunities that are convenient for all of the participants. Cominco plans group-oriented sessions around the needs of the group (DeBiasio et al., 1999). This is the process they use:

1. They send out an interest bulletin with a description of the session, including its length, and a deadline for sign-up.

2. They check with all who are interested to determine the time and day that works for them. The session date will be one that works for all participants.

3. An outside instructor/facilitator must be able to work around the learners' schedules.

The Cominco learning team believes this removes one of the biggest obstacles to getting people involved in learning. While it may feel like a juggling act to the person who has to do the scheduling, it is very customer focused. Their motto is "If we can, you can!" In other words, if we can find a time that works for all of you, you will have more opportunities for learning.

Developing Learning Space

In Phase 3, the learning space was identified. Concurrent with the development of learning opportunities, the space should be made ready for use. Whether you create a stand-alone learning center or develop one within an existing space, count on delays in handling the details. Something always seems to happen—the electricity cannot be hooked up as scheduled, the equipment does not arrive on time, and so on. By making allowances for delays in your plans, neither your team nor your potential learners will be disappointed.

Planning and Implementing Marketing Strategy

How will employees find out about your learning system? What do they need to know about the learning system? When do they need to know it? When you have answered these questions, create a timeline for disseminating information. The marketing strategy should generate excitement about learning and the opportunities that are being developed.

You may want to create a logo for your learning system that could be used on all promotional materials and handouts. Perhaps an in-house graphics department could assist with the design.

Listed below are some of the more traditional methods of publicizing the new system:

- Articles in the organization newsletter. Run these on a regular basis during the planning process to provide information about specific plans, system completion date, learning staff, and so on.

- Publish a list of various employee learning activities online on an employee news network and update it daily on the organization's electronic bulletin board.

- Create a monthly or quarterly learning newsletter that focuses exclusively on learning activities.

- Make posters about the learning system in general and the specific opportunities, and post them on bulletin boards.

- Pairs of learning system design team members could speak at departmental meetings.

- A learning staff person could attend shift or crew leader talks to facilitate conversations on learning.

- Host informal brown-bag lunches to answer questions about the system.

- Design promotional materials such as pencils or bookmarks.

- Plan tours of the learning center for a grand opening. Involve family members. Invite the local press.

Presentations about the learning system should be informal and fun. Stress brushing up or regaining lost skills in order to avoid intimidating some potential learners. Focus on the need for evolving skills and life-long learning in the future, and emphasize the benefits for individuals who engage in learning. Presenters should highlight the personal approach of the learning system—that this system is designed to provide learning opportunities that fit individual needs. Explain that adult learning is different from primary- and secondary-school learning and that the system is designed to be user-friendly. Make sure learning staff are available for one-on-one discussions and guarantee that all conversations are confidential.

Provide giveaways in the employee break room and at the information sessions. Gehl Company distributes little magnets with learning-related sayings, such as "Attitude: What the mind can conceive and believe, it can achieve" (Harlaquinn et al., 1999).

You will also want to develop brochures or flyers about specific learning opportunities. These could be one-page handouts or a catalog of opportunities broken down by system component (individual, peer, group), learning context (formal, semiformal, nonformal, informal), learning outcome, or any other method that appears workable.

Planning and Implementing a Support System

Individual learning in organizations cannot sustain itself in a systematic way without some support from the entire organization. The learning system must be integrated with other systems. Mechanisms include tying learning to performance evaluations, including it as a factor in a pay system, and ensuring that the managerial and supervisory staff are committed to learning. Do not expect to implement all of these suggestions at once; instead, create a game plan and address the items one by one.

Recruitment To create an organization filled with people who are learning, recruit action-oriented employees who are self-motivated, resourceful problem solvers, and willing to take risks. The key is to strive for a balance between learning and task efficiency.

When hiring new employees, look for those who, in addition to their other abilities, are learners. You may be able to discern this quality by asking questions such as "Can you tell me about a time when you had a problem working with someone else? How did you handle it?" or "Please share with me something new you have learned in the past year. How did you learn it?" You may need to suggest that learning does not happen only in classes.

Financial Support Much of the learning in your system will be done in a semiformal, nonformal, or informal manner, which requires less money than formal training and is more likely to take place in the workplace; but financial support is still important. Financial incentives can help get people into a learning mode. You may also need formal learning institutions for some learning needs.

- *Personal development funds:* To get people interested in learning, some companies have created a fund to support any kind of learning. These funds should have features such as

  —A set amount of money per employee per year

  —Minimal rules for use

  —A simple reimbursement form

  —A designated administrator/coordinator

A personal development fund is generally a small amount of money that must be used during the course of a year; if it is not used, it is lost. It could be as little as $100 per year per employee. This money may be spent on any materials or classes as long as they lead to learning. The activity does not have to be work related. In one organization, people have used their funds for books on cooking techniques, videotapes on bow hunting, and classes on flower arranging. The only requirement is that fund users must somehow use their minds. Others have applied their funds to more work-related issues, such as a computer class at a local community college, a subscription to a technical magazine, or textbooks for a class on psychology. Money that remains in the fund at the end of the year does not accumulate, but every employee begins the new year with $100.

The rules for use of a personal development fund should be minimal. Some suggested rules include

—Available to employees with a specified minimum hours of service

—Activities or items must lead to learning

—Not for physical activities

—Reimbursement with proof of purchase, or, alternatively, with application or order form submitted for payment

As shown in Figure 4, the form for reimbursement should be simple. The purpose of such funds is to get people involved in learning—to at least get started and see that learning can be fun. Offering support for a variety of learning activities helps people realize that taking classes is not the only way to learn. This type of entry-level program often leads to involvement in additional company-sponsored learning opportunities. Most people first use the fund for an item of personal interest. More than half use it the second time for a work-related purpose.

In a similar program, the State of Ohio and the Ohio Civil Service Employees Association (OCSEA) operate a joint program that allows employees $1,000 per year, which can be used to attend a conference, seminar, or workshop from an accredited group (Rice, Bell, and West, 1999).

Congratulations on your decision to grow through the Personal Development Fund. The fund provides resources that can truly advance your learning and development process. To receive funds, it is important that you read and answer all of the following items. Thanks for your cooperation.

1. Is this development request

    ___ related to current work?

    ___ related to future career?

    ___ of personal interest?

2. Please give a brief description of how this resource will help you to grow:

    _____

    _____

    _____

    _____

    _____

3. Cost: Attach receipt or other record of payment.

    Title: _____

    Cost: _____ Date (if class, seminar, or conference): _____

    Circle type of resource you are purchasing:

    Book   Magazine   Audio/Videocassette   Seminar/Conference   Class

4. Date: _____ Signature: _____

    Facility: _____ Print Name: _____

    Department: _____ Shift: _____

Figure 4   Personal Development Fund Form

- *Continuing education funds:* Many organizations have some form of continuing education fund. One survey found that 47.5% of 3,358 businesses surveyed offered continuing education funds (Lynch and Black, 1996). A continuing education fund pays tuition for any employee who is attending a degree-granting institution.

Continuing education funds vary widely as to the rules for use and amount of money available. They will often reimburse employees for up to 100% of their tuition. Sometimes a person must receive a grade of A to be reimbursed 100%; a lower grade garners lesser amounts. Some continuing education funds pay for textbooks.

There are many varieties of continuing education funds. Some companies have adopted the philosophy that any type of learning is valuable to the organization, whether it is work related or not. In these cases, the company will pay for non-work-related classes. I met a young man in a machining company who was taking Russian language classes at a local college. The tuition and books were covered 100% by his company's continuing education fund.

Some companies pay in excess of 100% for a grade of A or B. For instance, Fowler Products Company reimburses 100% of tuition for a grade of C, 150% for a B, and 200% for an A (Wood and Gilbert, 1996). The State of Ohio/OCSEA program pays for classes in advance. Their policy is to pay for a course only once. Employees who fail a course do not have to pay back the money, but they will not receive funds to try again. Other companies require employees to reimburse them through a payroll deduction if they fail to complete the class.

The Redmond Group uses revenue to determine the amount of money available for learning (Galagan, Barron, and Salopek, 1999). For each billable employee hour, a set amount of money goes into the learning fund; for unbillable hours, a smaller amount is set aside. The company expects to spend $5,000–$6,000 per employee per year. It does not hesitate to deny requests for funding if it appears there will be little learning involved or if the proposed learning does not support the company's goal. Staff members who want to take classes, go to conferences, or buy books must attend a staff meeting and explain why they need the knowledge and how it supports the company's mission. The staff then votes on whether or not to release the funds. If the expenditure is approved, learners must share their new knowledge with coworkers at the conclusion of their learning experience.

The State of Ohio and the OCSEA negotiated a continuing education fund into their contract (Rice, Bell, and West, 1999). It provides for up to $4,250 for education per year per employee. This sum includes $2,500 for tuition, $750 for computer literacy, and $1,000 for professional development conferences. Use of the fund is self-directed, but guidance and support are available on request. The only caveat is that the learning must somehow be applicable to a job in the state civil service. The program is funded through a contribution of 5 cents per member from the OCSEA and 10 cents per employee from the state. Courses are paid for through a voucher arrangement with the state's accredited educational institutions.

The United Automobile Workers (UAW) and General Motors (GM) have created a Tuition Assistance Program (TAP). This program provides prepaid tuition assistance of up to $3,800 per year for active workers, $8,000 per year for laid-off workers, and $1,000 per year for retirees. At United Technologies Corporation, continuing education funds cover tuition, books, and fees for undergraduate or graduate degrees and may be used for coursework that is not work related (McCain and Pantazis, 1997). The company also pays full- and part-time employees for half the time they spend attending classes during their normal working hours. In addition, United Technologies has added a reward component of 50 shares of company stock for the completion of a bachelor's degree and 25 shares for the completion of an associate's degree.

In 1989, the Steelworkers Union created an Institute for Career Development. The union negotiated a contribution from the steel companies of 10 cents per hour for each union member. The institute offers a variety of learning opportunities, such as a tutoring program to assist members in passing work-related skills tests and obtaining their GEDs. One participant commented, "I'm doing the whole nine yards and I love it. The more knowledge I have, the better I'll be about steel and the world" (Sunoo, 1999, p. 3). Another steelworker was able to obtain 65 college credits through the institute's distance learning program.

Some organizations require a minimum length of employment—90 days to a year seems to be common. Others make funds available immediately to new employees and those who are laid off or on disability. Some also provide continuing education for seasonal workers. You may want to make the use of these funds part of the personal development planning process. A simple application form such as the one shown in Figure 5 may be helpful in administering the program.

A Chinese proverb states that when "you teach you learn twice." Some companies require fund users to give a presentation at a brown-bag lunch or write a report on what they have learned for the company's learning resource center. (See also the discussion of learning centers in Chapter 4). Individuals who do this find they often learn as much from their own presentations or written reports as from a class. Others then have the opportunity to benefit from the participant's education as well.

Some organizations offer continuing education funds to family members. Johnsonville Sausage created a scholarship program for the spouses and children of employees. It provides $2,000 per year for four-year colleges or universities and $1,000 per year for two-year institutions. Not everyone who applies automatically receives a scholarship. Selections are made by an employee committee and are based on previous academic achievement, leadership in school or community participation, and a statement of career goals. Scholarships are renewable for the duration of the educational program.

• *Paid educational leave:* The UAW-GM educational program provides paid educational leave for a study program that covers the history of the automobile industry and examination of current trends. It concludes with an action planning segment in which participants develop ideas for improvements at their workplaces.

Another program places 1.5% of gross payroll contributions into an educational trust, which can provide up to a two-year leave and a maximum of $10,000 per year to cover tuition, pension, health care, and books.

Congratulations on your decision to grow through the Continuing Education Fund. The fund provides resources that can truly advance your learning and development process. To receive funds, it is important that you read and answer all of the following items. Thanks for your cooperation.

Name _____ Department _____

Work phone _____ Home phone _____

School name and location _____

Term start date _____

I am enrolling in the following program (check one):

❑ Continuing education ❑ Associate degree ❑ Bachelor degree

❑ Graduate degree ❑ Certificate program

How will this course assist you with your Personal Development Plan?

_____

_____

_____

Course information

	Course name	Course no.	Tuition	Gen. fees	Lab fees	Total
1.						
2.						
3.						

Figure 5　Continuing Education Fund Request Form

For targeted jobs in areas with skill shortages, General Motors' Work-to-Work program provides full salary and benefits plus tuition and book expenses. The only employees who are eligible are those currently working in an area that is slated for downsizing. The person must pass a selection test demonstrating ability in the targeted area and must commit to staying in the new job for a specified period of time. To ensure that the skills will be directly applicable to the job, the company's partnering committee works closely with the educational institutions involved. A similar program could be developed even when downsizing is not an issue: There may be a labor shortage in some areas of your organization; creating an incentive program for employees can be a great way to get people trained.

• *Personal computer purchase program:* Johnsonville Sausage offers employees interest-free loans ranging from $650 to $2,000 for the purchase of a personal computer or specific components for an existing system. Employees may select equipment independently or with the assistance of the program coordinator, who is a member of the information systems staff. However, after the purchase is made, the company does not provide technical support for the system.

The loan is repaid through payroll deductions and repayment must be completed within two years. If the employee leaves the company, any remaining balance is deducted from the final paycheck.

Reward Systems

Reward systems are not just monetary—they can be intrinsic or extrinsic. Intrinsic rewards are self-generated and usually are not visible. Over time, learning itself can become an intrinsic reward. Extrinsic rewards are provided by someone other than the learner, and include items such as compensation or other forms of recognition.

A pay system will not motivate people to want to learn, but it may help them begin the process. It certainly will not discourage learning and it may act as reinforcement and support. The pay system at YSI, Inc., stipulates that employees acquire two learning units per year (Honold, 1999). The learning units are loosely defined to allow the employee a certain amount of latitude in meeting the requirement. If an employee can demonstrate that he or she has learned something, the experience will qualify.

Recognizing learners for their accomplishments can be a tremendous boost, particularly for those who are just getting into the learning mode. Some examples include

• 150 of the best knowledge sharers at Buckman Laboratories received resort vacations, new laptop computers, and invitations to a presentation by Tom Peters (Pan and Scarborough, 1998).

- Learning systems participants received free T-shirts.

- Learners received compensatory time off.

- Bostrom Seating of Piedmont, Alabama, flies graduates of the in-house GED program to the company headquarters in Chicago for a graduation ceremony (Millner et al., 1999).

- 3M created a number of awards to recognize innovation. The Golden Step Award is given for achievement in sales with a new product. The Circle of Technical Excellence Award celebrates innovative technical contributions. Carlton Society membership signifies a more exclusive level of technical contribution. The Pathfinder Program honors teams that develop new products (Brand, 1998).

Similar recognition programs could be created for your organization. A note of caution, however—while extrinsic rewards may help to get people into a learning mode, at some point they cease to be of value. It is rather like Maslow's hierarchy of needs: Maslow (1943) suggested that basic needs motivate until they are fulfilled, at which point safety needs become the motivator, and then belonging, followed by ego/status, and ultimately self-actualization. As people become learners, the lower-level needs, which tend to be extrinsic, are less important. Learning in itself is a motivator. When extrinsic rewards are provided to a person who is no longer at that level of motivation, they can be viewed negatively.

Some organizations are equally direct about the consequences of noninvolvement in learning. For example, the leadership of Buckman Laboratories wrote a letter to employees who did not fulfill the sharing component of the learning system, indicating that opportunities would no longer be available to them if they continued to avoid participation (Pan and Scarborough, 1998).

Performance Development Planning

Performance development planning reinforces learning by allowing people to design their own learning process. It can augment or even replace performance evaluations. Evaluation is judgmental and based on history; planning is developmental and builds for tomorrow. Development planning should be woven into the learning system. You might institute a policy requiring a current development plan before an employee can accept a promotion or a new position. Be sure that the plan derives from thorough understanding of an individual's learning desires and is not just another hoop employees have to jump through on their way to promotions.

Dual Career Ladders

Some companies, like 3M, create dual career ladders—in technical and management/leadership tracks (Brand, 1998). In the technical track, employees do not have to manage people; they can focus their creative energies on innovation. Dual career ladders may support learning by allowing learners to focus on their strengths and continue to learn rather than become frustrated because they cannot advance without taking on roles and responsibilities that do not match their skills, abilities, or attributes.

Supporting the Supervisor and Manager Role in Learning

Transforming traditional managers and supervisors into coaches and developers of people requires a change in leadership methods. Leaders may need assistance learning to coach and mentor. Research has shown that a traditional training approach will not work (Cunningham, 1999; Fisher, Merron, and Torbert, 1987; McAll, Lombardo, and Srooisson, 1988; Tetrault, Schriesheim, and Neider, 1989). Training rarely leads to behavioral change. To quote Ralph Stayer (1998), CEO of Johnsonville Foods, "If you always do what you've always done, you'll always get what you've already got."

In asking people to learn to lead, coach, and develop, it is important that the process itself be a model for what you are asking them to do (Spreitzer and Quinn, 1996). Therefore, rather than employing a strict presentation mode in which the trainer is responsible for creating the program's content, the trainer should be more of a facilitator, whose responsibility is to lay out the broad-based content of the workshop and keep the process on track. The participants should determine the specific content and take responsibility for developing themselves.

In the past, learning in organizations has not been intentionally supported. Without realizing it, managers and supervisors may put a damper on learning. If learning is to be a key element of an organization's system, it must be balanced with the need to provide a product or service. People in leadership roles may require new skills, such as facilitation and coaching, to support the process. Suggestions for developing facilitation and coaching skills are included in Chapter 11.

Supporting Learning Staff

An organization's learning staff could also benefit from support processes. Are there other companies in your area that are focused on learning? A support network would allow staff from those in your geographic area to meet regularly in a learning format to discuss ideas, successes, and the challenges involved in creating a different approach to learning in organizations.

Developing Alliances

One of the problems you may face when selecting components for your learning system is a lack of resources. Develop alliances with other businesses, educational institutions, or government programs as a way of expanding your capabilities. Corning partners with outside groups to sponsor degree programs and what they call "commodities" courses, or high-demand courses (McCain and Pantazis, 1997). Corning confirms that its partners value learning in a similar way.

In addition to partnering, you may augment your resources in the following ways:

- Develop a network. A learning network allies small businesses with one another to share the cost of bringing in resources. Four small companies could hire one learning resource person who splits his or her time four ways.

- Use subcontractors. You do not have to present all the workshops or design all the learning opportunities. Contract with local educational institutions or consultants to design and implement them for you.

- Ask leaders or other employees to facilitate learning. They will set an example for others and learn in the process. Leaders then fill three roles: model, coach, and partner.

- Involve suppliers and customers in learning programs.

Phase 5: Implementation and Improvement

Everything is now ready to go. Some of the learning opportunities are already in place. A kickoff event, such as a festive open house, would serve to notify everyone in the organization that the process is under way.

During an open house, present a small learning experience that is easy and enlightening, such as the Learn How You Learn Checklist, in Chapter 6. Afterward, provide each participant with a written description of the learning styles indicated. The checklist might entice people into doing a more in-depth personal assessment. Offer every attendee the opportunity to register for a door prize, which should be fun but related to learning.

Once the system is up and running, it is time to initiate the processes of measuring, documenting, and improving.

Measurement and Documentation

In today's business world, there is an emphasis on measuring the impact of training. Some companies commit a certain percentage of an employee's work time to educational endeavors. Corning attempts to have employees' spend 5% of their time in work-related training (McCain and Pantazis, 1997). Wainwright Industries does not require it but spends approximately 7% of its payroll on training. This approach allows companies to quantify training. However, there are drawbacks: The number of courses offered, the amount of time devoted to those courses, and the money spent in providing the courses do not reveal whether learning has taken place. This approach to learning may lead to an undesirable result—spending time and resources on classroom learning just because we are able to measure it.

As we have seen, many learning opportunities occur while people are working. How are these experiences quantified? It is virtually impossible. If we measure only official events, we miss much of the learning that takes place; we may concentrate on formal training instead of creating a context for learning within the workplace—which, research suggests, is where most learning takes place.

To date, I have seen no comprehensive measure for learning. Measurement is difficult because results are so intangible. Organizations that focus successfully on learning do it because they believe it is the right thing to do. They believe there is a connection between people who are learning and the bottom line. They do not attempt to quantify the process; they just do it (Pfeffer and Veiga, 1999).

Although you may not be able to measure your learning system in a traditional sense, there are ways to determine how much learning is occurring and thereby provide evidence of the system's effectiveness.

- Conduct face-to-face evaluations, either one-on-one or in group meetings. Ask open-ended questions, or questions that encourage people to express their feelings, such as "What did you learn that was new?" "Was there anything that caused you discomfort in your learning? Why were you uncomfortable?" Ask analytical questions, such as "Why do you think that happened?" Engage others: "Does anyone have a different perspective?" This approach might be challenging initially, but as learners develop skills and self-confidence, they will offer assessments more readily.

- To evaluate the whole learning culture, ask questions of learners and managers as well as the learning staff. Marquardt (1999) suggests queries such as "How can our learnings be applied to the organization? Our work group? Are we learning from our mistakes?"

- Examine all the development plans. Be sure employees are not filling out development forms just for the sake of having them. To guard against this tendency, check the plans for thoughtfulness and thoroughness and compare development plans with attainment of or movement toward the stated goals.

- Document learning by asking participants to describe what their learning has meant to them, either in a written report or in a taped interview. This approach—having participants determine their own level of learning—is more in line with adult learning philosophy.

We have discussed various approaches to supporting a learning system. Some may be useful to you and some may not be. What is critical is your awareness of the support mechanisms you have in place for your learning system.

Continuing Development of a Learning Support System

As you go about designing your learning support system, you may want to address each of the items covered in this chapter. You may identify others that were not mentioned but are relevant to your organization. If so, incorporate them into your overall system. Exercise 2 provides a checklist to assist you in this task.

Improvement

Your learning system may be designed, but your work is not over. The programs must be reviewed on an ongoing basis. Are they meeting the needs of the organization and the people within it? Some learning opportunities begin with great promise and achieve great success but grow stale over time and no longer lead to learning. For instance, the learners at Johnsonville Sausage found the Scan, Clip, and Review process described in Chapter 9 quite useful for about six months. After that, it became routine and the program was discontinued. Perhaps "put on the shelf" is a better description, as it may be used again, possibly with a different group of learners or even with the same group after a period of time.

Your learning system design team may assume the ongoing role of providing suggestions for continual review, update, and revision of your system. The learning system design will never be complete. To survive, it must be a living, learning entity.

Ongoing Marketing of Learning

Even after the learning system is functioning smoothly, the work of marketing the system remains a constant, ongoing process. Employees have other things on their minds and will need to be reminded of existing opportunities and informed of new ones as they are developed. If your system gets large enough, you might want to create a catalog of available opportunities.

Newsletters could include testimonials or examples of the positive results of learning, written by learning resources staff or the learners themselves. For some individuals, the act of writing the article might prove to be another mechanism for learning.

Be creative. Show that learning can be fun. Involve departments in the marketing process. If they meet on a regular basis, try to get 10 minutes on the agenda. Bring in a short, enjoyable learning exercise. Take the opportunity to pass out flyers on currently available learning opportunities.

EXERCISE 2: CHECKLIST FOR SUPPORT SYSTEMS

Element	IN PLACE?	Description of Support in Place
Systems	Yes / No	
Recruitment		
Financial support		
Reward systems: Compensation		
Reward systems: Recognition		
Dual career ladder		
Performance development planning		
Staff Support	Yes / No	
Supervisors/managers		
Learning resources		

Even if you have not created an entire learning system, marketing what you have in simple ways, such as company newsletter articles, will encourage people to try out the activities that are available.

PART 3

THE LEARNING TOOLBOX: A Compendium of Tools, Strategies, and Resources

The only person who is educated is the one who has learned how to learn . . . and change.

CARL ROGERS

Creating a planned approach to individual learning in an organization is not easy. Skeptics will ask, "Why should we invest in learning for people who work in a factory or who are on the phone all day long?" Some will not understand how a semiformal, nonformal, or informal approach to learning could have a positive impact on the organization. In fact, learning is happening every day, regardless of what we want. Wise management staff will take the time to create a process that capitalizes on that learning. As a result of such efforts, the organization will function more efficiently, and its employees can experience a greater level of satisfaction with their work.

Approaches to Learning Opportunities

Learning is about knowing ourselves—in knowing ourselves, we are able to broaden our learning capacity. Individual employees have different attitudes about learning and different learning styles. They may be at different levels of development. They may be learning alone, with a peer, or in groups. Therefore, the learning program needs to develop opportunities to suit each variation. The beginning phase is simply getting people into a learning mode. Once employees are open to learning, the next challenge is to continue the process—individually, in one-on-one relationships, and in groups—by integrating learning into work.

Chapters 6 and 7 focus mainly on the individual. Chapter 6 addresses the challenge of getting people into a learning mode—being open to learning and eventually searching for their own opportunities to learn. It describes approaches that enable people to develop knowledge, skill, courage, self-awareness, sensitivity to others, and perseverance. Initially, the process may entail learning tools that have little apparent value to the organization. The key, though, is to get people started. Any kind of learning that occurs in the workplace will naturally expand into areas that affect the job and the organization. If it is part of an overall learning strategy, it will have a much greater impact.

Chapter 7 emphasizes ongoing individual learning. It describes how to create opportunities that will move learners beyond scheduled learning activities to the less structured process of learning to learn, so that they can take advantage of learning in almost any situation.

The next three chapters are concerned with different styles and approaches to learning in the workplace. Chapter 8 focuses on learning in one-on-one relationships, and Chapter 9 covers learning in a group setting. Chapter 10 addresses ways of integrating learning into daily work.

Chapter 11 provides ideas for those in leadership positions who want to help their employees become learners.

Format of Selections

The following chapters offer a compendium of learning opportunities to accommodate various needs. You may experiment with them, and then tailor them to your organization, your employees, and the changing needs of both. In choosing appropriate learning opportunities, you should consider the following factors.

Stage of Learner

- *Stage 1:* Learner is minimally self-directed; facilitator is responsible for content and process

- *Stage 2:* Learner is moderately self-directed; facilitator and learner are both responsible for content and process

- *Stage 3:* Learner is able to explore learning needs independently; facilitator acts as guide and resource when needed

- *Stage 4:* Learner is self-directed; facilitator's role is limited as learner takes control of his or her own learning

Context for Learning

- *Informal:* Outside or inside formal organization; self-directed

- *Nonformal:* Organized, but outside formal, established system; may be facilitated or self-directed

- *Semiformal:* Organized inside formal, established system; facilitated, not directed

- *Formal:* Inside formal, established system; led by expert

Learning Style Accommodated

- *Activist:* Open-minded and enthusiastic experimentation

- *Pragmatist:* Down-to-earth problem solver

- *Theorist:* Logical and analytical

- *Reflector:* Cautious and observant

Outcome of Learning

- New knowledge

- New attitude and/or values

- Skill development—physical, mental, or social

- Aspiration

An ideal learning system addresses learners at different stages, in different contexts, with different learning styles, and with needs for different outcomes. This format will assist you in choosing which learning approaches to implement.

Learning Resources Role

The role of a learning resources staff person was discussed in Chapter 4. This heading provides a brief description of the work the staff person must perform to implement the learning opportunities.

6

Methods for Developing Interest in Learning and Self-Knowledge

We are in the midst of a fundamental revolution in learning; yet we still think of training through traditional pipelines, [and] certifying institutions instead of individuals.

MARY L. MCCAIN AND CYNTHIA PANTAZIS
Responding to Workplace Change

Before learning can become a strategic organizational tool, employees must first engage in it and find value in it. To be effective learners, employees must understand themselves—they will then gain more from learning activities. However, some may not be ready to take that big a step. They may need to ease into the learning process. This section contains specific learning tools—processes that will guide people toward self-knowledge—and systemic and structural mechanisms to support new learning.

This chapter presents methods, strategies, and tools designed to help individuals determine their goals, learning styles, decision-making approaches, and values and then create a plan for learning and development. This may be accomplished by a formal personal development workshop or through nonformal methods, such as individualized personal development coaching.

A cautionary note on employees who enter the learning mode: <u>As people begin to learn, they may feel some discomfort</u>. This is part of the process. <u>Without discomfort, there is little learning.</u> To borrow a phrase from athletes in training—"no pain, no gain." In this case, <u>the pain is</u> not physical, it is mental and emotional. It might be wise to recognize the possibility of a new learner's sense of unease and be prepared to deal with it if it arises.

When Johnsonville Sausage first developed its learning system there were a number of people who did not think it was valuable for them. Leaders decided not to force employees into learning but instead to provide opportunities that would give these employees a chance to overcome some of their misgivings while they eased into the learning mode. The company posted a sign-up sheet for people who were interested in working on improving the quality of life at the workplace. A group of approximately eight people met with a facilitator to brainstorm issues that prevented the company from being the best place to work. Then the group prioritized problems based on impact and their own ability to resolve them.

The group's first project was the food in the break-room vending machines. Many employees who had only a half hour for lunch often resorted to the vending machines and were dissatisfied with the selection. The facilitator asked the group to suggest a solution. They thought it would be best to offer different food altogether. As they were discussing what items should be available, a disagreement broke out over whether one kind of sandwich was better than another. On reflection, the group decided that if there was already disagreement within their small group, there probably would be disagreement in the larger organization. To ensure that they obtained food their coworkers would enjoy, they conducted an informal survey over the next couple of weeks.

At the next group meeting, committee members listed the food they wanted in the vending machines. The next step was to contact the company that provided the vending service. Initially, the group wanted the facilitator to do this, but, after further discussion, they decided that because she did not use the machines, perhaps one of the group members should call.

The person who volunteered was an hourly employee. When she contacted the vending machine company she was told that she did not have the clout to make the call and the company would prefer to deal with a manager. She reported this response to the team, and they decided they did not want to do business with a company that treated people in that way. They investigated further and found another vending machine company that was more than willing to deal with the employee and provide the food the group wanted.

This process was designed to help people solve a problem situation in which they were directly involved. It was like a hands-on Decision Making 101 course. The group worked together to figure out how to resolve the issue. They learned in the process. After being exposed to learning through an experience that resulted in a positive outcome for them, several members of the group sought out additional learning opportunities.

Selecting Learning Tools
to Get Employees into the Learning Mode

As you go about selecting or creating tools to help employees enter the learning mode, you will want to vary your approach to accommodate different learning contexts, stages of learning, learning styles, and targeted outcomes. Table 3 on the following pages lists all the learning tools outlined in this chapter and is designed to assist with that process.

The personal development planning process should help get employees into the learning mode. It will enable those who are already open to learning to be more effective and efficient in the future. Once these objectives have been met, the challenge is to maintain the learning process. Ongoing individual learning will be addressed in Chapter 7.

Easing into the Learning Mode

Many people do not have fond memories of sitting in classrooms during their high school or college days. They did it because they had to do it, not by choice. As a result, any mention of learning may intimidate them or cause automatic resistance. Therefore, it is important to create mechanisms to ease them into learning a bit at a time. Perhaps the easiest way to accomplish this is to begin with something that benefits them.

TABLE 3 INDIVIDUAL LEARNING SELECTION

	Stage for Learner	Context for Learning	Complementary Learning Style(s)	Outcome of Learning	Work Related?
EASING INTO THE LEARNING MODE					
Problem Resolution as a Mechanism for Active Learning	1, 2, 3, 4	Semiformal, Nonformal	Activist, Pragmatist, Reflector	Knowledge, Skill	Yes
Personal Development Funds	1, 2, 3, 4	Formal, Semiformal, Nonformal, or Informal	Activist, Pragmatist, Theorist, Reflector	Knowledge, Attitude/Values, Skill, Aspiration	Possibly
Continuing Education Funds	1, 2, 3, 4	Formal, Semiformal	Pragmatist, Theorist, Reflector	Knowledge, Skill	Yes
Paid Educational Leave	3, 4	Formal, Semiformal	Pragmatist, Theorist, Reflector	Knowledge, Attitude/Values, Skill, Aspiration	Yes
Personal Computer Purchase Program	1, 2, 3, 4	Informal, Nonformal	Activist, Pragmatist, Theorist, Reflector	Skill	Possibly
Computer Enrichment Training	1, 2, 3	Formal	Activist, Pragmatist,	Knowledge, Skill	No

KNOWLEDGE OF SELF

Clarifying Essential Personal Values	1, 2	Semiformal	Activist, Pragmatist, Reflector	Knowledge, Attitude/Values	Possibly
Learning Lifeline–Depicting How People Learn	1, 2, 3	Semiformal	Activist, Pragmatist, Reflector	Knowledge, Attitude/Values	No
Instruments for Determining Learning Style	1, 2, 3	Formal	Activist, Pragmatist, Reflector	Knowledge, Attitude/Values	No
Instruments for Determining What Motivates Learners	1, 2, 3	Semiformal	Activist, Pragmatist, Reflector	Knowledge, Attitude/Values	No
Instruments for Understanding Perceptions and Tendencies	1, 2, 3	Formal	Activist, Pragmatist, Reflector	Knowledge, Attitude/Values	No
Current Skills Inventory	1, 2, 3	Semiformal	Activist, Pragmatist, Reflector	Knowledge, Attitude/Values	Yes
Comprehensive Personal Development Workshop	1, 2, 3	Formal, Semiformal	Activist, Pragmatist, Reflector	Knowledge, Attitude/Values, Skill, Aspiration	Yes
Individual Personal Development Counseling	1, 2, 3	Nonformal	Activist, Pragmatist, Theorist, Reflector	Knowledge, Attitude/Values, Skill, Aspiration	Yes
Self-Study in Personal Development	2, 3	Nonformal	Pragmatist, Theorist, Reflector	Knowledge, Attitude/Values, Skill, Aspiration	Yes
Software for Competency Evaluation	2, 3	Semiformal	Activist, Pragmatist	Knowledge, Aspiration	Yes
360° Feedback–Learning How Others Perceive Us	3, 4	Nonformal, Informal	Pragmatist, Theorist, Reflector	Knowledge, Attitude/Values, Aspiration	Yes

Learning Tools

To enter a learning mode, individual learners may need tools to facilitate their learning. A process for problem resolution or financial support may provide just what is needed.

Problem Resolution as a Mechanism for Active Learning

Stage for learner: 1, 2, 3, or 4

Context for learning: Semiformal, Nonformal

Learning styles best accommodated: Activist, Pragmatist, Reflector

Outcome of learning: Knowledge, Skill Development (mental and social)

Learning resources role: Facilitate or find facilitator for process.

Select an issue of concern to employees or bring together a group to identify one. The group may be composed of volunteers or, sometimes, specific individuals may be asked to get involved. Resolving a problem is often a great way to turn negative employees into part of the solution. This positive experience may convince them to support the new learning system.

Once the issue is identified, determine who else will be affected by any changes and ask for their input or involvement in the process. Determine the best resolution and implement it. Revise if necessary. It is important that the person who facilitates the process does not implement it. With action comes a sense of ownership. This exercise will be most valuable if the ownership of the solution rests with the learners.

This kind of action learning process can be implemented in any organization. The project can be workplace related, as in the example given above, or it can relate more directly to work. The people involved in the process must have the authority to resolve the issue. Being responsible only for investigation and not for resolution diminishes the value of the learning. If the group's plan is altered by an external party or not implemented at all, the learning value may be erased.

Providing Financial Support for Learning

Stage for learner: 1, 2, 3, or 4

Context for learning: Varies based on use

Learning styles best accommodated: Varies based on use

Outcome of learning: Varies based on use

Learning resources role: Develop, advertise, and administer program

- *Personal Development Funds:* Provide a small amount of money to pay for books or continuing education courses.

- *Continuing Education Funds:* Pay for classes at a formal educational institution such as a technical college or university.

- *Paid Educational Leave:* Offer sabbaticals, such as those often available for educators. Educational leave allows employees to take time off from work to attend full-time educational programs. (Please note: This type of learning opportunity is most valuable for advanced stage learners.)

- *Personal Computer Purchase Program:* Provide money for the purchase of a personal computer, accessories, and software.

- *Computer Enrichment Training:* Provide financial support for programs that focus on computer and software skills.

These programs give people an opportunity to learn about subjects that are important to them. Employees are likely to view such programs as beneficial and nonintrusive. By participating, they may begin to feel more at ease about entering a learning mode.

Knowledge of Self

In *Type Talk* (Kroeger and Thuesen, 1988), a book that helps people understand some of their natural preferences, Charles Seashore says, "Know thyself. What will the neighbors think?" (p. 1). His point is that we not only must know ourselves but also understand how others perceive us. In doing so, we can become more effective individuals. Therefore, an early step in creating opportunities for individual learning is to develop the learner's self-awareness or self-knowledge.

To be an effective learner, each person should be able to answer the following questions:

- Where have I been?

- What skills do I already possess?

- How do I learn?

- What are my values?

- What learning experiences have I had to date?

It is important to acknowledge past learning. Some individuals embarking on a learning effort will feel intimidated. They may have attended school and perhaps received degrees. They may have completed training programs. Often, though, they have not consciously thought through what they really know and believe. They also may not realize that they have already acquired many skills and much knowledge— through informal learning. Understanding provides a base on which to build future learning.

- Where do I want to go?

- What do I not know now that I want or feel I need to know?

- What is my future in my current job?

- My career?

- My personal life?

Learners need to have some idea of what they want to learn. The goal for learning does not necessarily have to be specific; however, it must be defined and understood, otherwise the process could resemble aimless wandering that does not lead to any real learning. Even the exploration of a new concept or career area takes place within certain parameters. Not all people want to grow out of their current jobs. It is all right to say, "I am perfectly happy in this job." A person who feels this way has two learning options: to learn within the current job or to focus on learning about personal interests outside of work. Either way, both the employee and the organization benefit because, by simply being in a learning mode, an individual will be more open to change. In addition, in today's economy, it is highly likely that this particular job may change or cease to exist in the future.

- What are my specific goals in each area?

- What do I want to learn to expand myself in my current job?

- What do I want to learn to increase my chances of attaining my career objective?

- What do I want to learn to make my personal life more fulfilling?

The answers to this set of questions help frame the content of future learning. As learning paths become focused, goals will also be clearer. When possible, articulate goals as part of the learning process.

- How will I reach my learning goal?

- What steps and specific actions will I take to reach my goal?

- What learning forums will be most effective for me?

Planning is a critical part of the transition to active learning. Traditionally, answers to this set of questions led to a class or a degree program. Because we are exploring less formal learning, the approach to gaining new knowledge will be tailored to the specific style of each individual.

- How will I know when I arrive at the level of learning to which I aspire?

Having a picture of success in mind, even if vague—and even if it changes later due to new knowledge—helps us visualize the ending phase of learning. This in turn regenerates the learning process. How do we answer the questions we have posed? While some will be able to take in a self-managed approach, many will need some level of assistance and support.

Clarifying Essential Personal Values

Stage for learner: 1 or 2

Context for learning: Semiformal

Learning styles best accommodated: Activist, Pragmatist, Reflector

Outcome of learning: Knowledge, Attitude/Values

Learning resources role: Facilitate program reflection.

The simplest approach to clarifying personal values is a chart like the one in Table 4, on page 100. On the left side of the chart, participants

TABLE 4   PERSONAL VALUES

BEHAVIOR	OPPOSITE	VALUE
1. Meeting starts late	Meeting starts on time	Respect for others' timeliness
2. Lying about reason for tardiness	Telling the truth	Honesty

list behaviors that makes them angry. In the center, they record the opposite behaviors, that is, conduct they value. In the right column, they list their core values that are violated by the behaviors listed on the left.

Of course, participants will express values in their own words. Sometimes, however, a variation in wording may indicate a difference in values. For example, in the first item in Table 4, the personal value could be listed as "respect for others" or "timeliness." Discussion with the individual would help clarify which value is more significant.

You may also purchase more rigorous assessment instruments to determine core values.

Learning Lifeline—Depicting How People Learn

Stage for learner: 1, 2, or 3

Context for learning: Semiformal

Learning styles best accommodated: Activist, Pragmatist, Reflector

Outcome of learning: Knowledge, Attitude/Values, Aspiration

Learning resources role: Facilitate process individually or in groups.

Ask participants to draw their learning lifelines with felt-tipped markers on easel sheets (blank newsprint pad). The lifeline does not have to be a straight line but may be any form that represents what and how they have learned throughout their lives. It may begin at birth or later. There may be a gap of a few years when no learning took place. The lifeline may be colorful or black and white. The level of artistic skill does not matter as long as the depiction represents the participants' ideas of their learning patterns up to the present.

Next, ask participants to present their completed learning lifelines to the rest of the group. You may want to set a time limit of 10 or 15 minutes per presentation. Doing this exercise for the first time helps people realize what has been of consequence in their past learning. New learning opportunities can pick up on themes of the past.

Some people may balk at this exercise; they may be self-conscious about their drawing ability. Reassure them that this is not about artistic ability but about thinking through the learning process and becoming more aware of it. The drawing may be as simple as a stick figure and a key phrase.

Instruments for Determining Learning Style

Stage for learner: 1, 2, or 3

Context for learning: Formal

Learning styles best accommodated: Activist, Pragmatist, Reflector

Outcome of learning: Knowledge, Attitude/Values

Learning resources role: Facilitate process individually or in groups.

When learners understand their own learning styles, as well as their strengths and weaknesses as learners, they can tailor activities to appeal to their strengths or to improve underdeveloped approaches. Some of the more common learning style instruments are the *Learning Style Inventories* by Kolb (1984; 1985), the *Learning Styles Questionnaire* by Honey and Mumford (1992), and the *Learning Type Measure* (Excel, 1999).

As discussed in Chapter 3, most of these instruments identify four main learning styles: the *converger*, who learns through abstract conceptualization and active experimentation; the *diverger*, who learns through concrete experience and reflective observation; the *assimilator*, who learns through abstract conceptualization and reflective observation; and the *accommodator*, who learns through concrete experience and active experimentation (Kolb, 1984). Honey and Mumford's learning styles (1992) are similar: The *activist* is open-minded and enthusiastic about learning; the *pragmatist* is a down-to-earth problem solver; the *theorist* is logical and analytical; and the *reflector* is cautious and observant in learning. These instruments are based on systematically reported data.

A simpler, though less reliable, approach to developing an understanding of learning styles is through an elementary checklist, such as the one in Exercise 3 on pages 103 and 104.

Instructions for completion of this checklist are

1. Ask participants to read each item and place a check mark next to the activities they feel they are likely to do.

2. When the checklist is completed, ask the participants to add up the number of check marks in each section. (There are two breaks on the form. I generally try to get the first two sections on one page and the third on a second page so people are less likely to realize the breaks until I point them out.)

Explain that each section represents a generalized learning style.

- Part 1 represents those who learn best by reading or other visual methods. People who learn best this way often find themselves drawn to books when they want to learn something new.

- Part 2 identifies those who learn best through listening or engaging in conversation. Learners who favor this style find they learn best in discussion with others or by listening to a speaker.

- Those who have the most check marks in Part 3 generally prefer a "learn by doing" approach. These learners have a tendency to jump into a project and experiment in a hands-on style when they are learning something new.

- Participants who find their check marks divided fairly evenly among the three sections may have a more versatile learning style or a tendency to learn different things in different ways.

This is just a quick method of assessing learning preferences. It is not scientifically valid and may not be accurate for every person. It is designed to get participants to think about how they learn best. If lack of funds is an issue, this may be a viable alternative to purchasing the more reliable instruments.

Instruments for Determining What Motivates Learners

Stage for learner: 1, 2, or 3

Context for learning: Semiformal

Learning styles best accommodated: Activist, Pragmatist, Reflector

EXERCISE 3: LEARNING STYLES CHECKLIST

LEARN HOW YOU LEARN

Each of us has a specific learning style, and we often want others to learn in the same way. It is important to be aware not only of how we learn but also of how others learn. Following is a simple, nonthreatening approach to determining learning styles.

Place a check mark next to each item that describes your preferences.

____ Like to keep written records

____ Typically read billboards while driving

____ Can put models together correctly using written directions

____ Follow written recipes easily when cooking

____ Review for a test by writing a summary

____ Express myself best by writing

____ Write on napkins in restaurants

____ Can put a bicycle together using written directions

____ Memorize a zip code by writing it down

____ Use visual images to remember names

____ Love to read

____ Write a note to compliment a friend

____ Plan the upcoming week by making a list

____ Prefer written directions from employer

____ Prefer reading/writing games like Scrabble

____ Prefer to have someone else read instructions when putting something together

____ Review for a test by reading notes aloud or by talking with others

____ Express myself best by talking

____ Talk aloud when working on a math problem

____ Would rather listen to a cassette than read the same material

____ Memorize a zip code by saying it

____ Use rhyming words to remember names

EXERCISE 3: LEARNING STYLES CHECKLIST (CONT'D)

____ Call on the telephone to compliment a friend

____ Plan the upcoming week by talking it over with someone

____ Talk to myself

____ Prefer oral directions from employer

____ Stop at a service station for directions in a strange city

____ Prefer talking/listening games

____ Keep up on news by listening to the radio

____ Can concentrate deeply on what another person is saying

____ Use free time for talking with others

____ Like to build things

____ Use the "just do it" approach to put a model together

____ Can distinguish items by touch when blindfolded

____ Learned the touch system rapidly in typing

____ Think gestures are an important part of communication

____ Move with music

____ Doodle and draw on any available paper

____ Enjoy the outdoors

____ Like to express myself through painting or dance

____ Move easily and am well coordinated

____ Spend a large amount of time on crafts and handiwork

____ Like to feel textures of objects, furnishings, or clothing

____ Prefer movement games to sit-down games

____ Find it fairly easy to keep physically fit

____ Can learn new physical skills quickly

____ Use free time for physical activities

Outcome of learning: Knowledge, Attitude/Values

Learning resources role: Facilitate process individually or in groups.

Several instruments or models can assist learners in determining what motivates them in their work, such as Edgar Schein's *Career Dynamics* (1978). Individuals can work through the self-assessment and then participate in a group discussion about the meaning of each career anchor.

Maslow's hierarchy of needs (1943; 1970), and/or Herzberg's satisfiers and demotivators (1968) can also be used as platforms for discussing motivation. Many people are already familiar with Maslow's work from supervisory management classes or basic psychology courses, which may contribute to some level of comfort with this discussion. Individuals or groups can examine each need (physiological, safety, belonging, self-esteem, and self-actualization) and the movement from one need to another as the previous need is fulfilled and ceases to act as a motivator. Participants may discern which needs currently motivate them and which ones used to motivate them. Workshop participants could observe how different people are motivated by different needs at different times in their lives. Herzberg's concepts of motivators and demotivators provide an avenue for complementary discussion. As both Maslow and Herzberg suggest that learning is a strong motivating need, their studies support the underlying premise of the Personal Development Planning Workshop.

Instruments for Understanding Perceptions and Tendencies

Stage for learner: 1, 2, or 3

Context for learning: Formal

Learning styles best accommodated: Activist, Pragmatist, Reflector

Outcome of learning: Knowledge, Attitude/Values

Learning resources role: Facilitate process individually or in groups.

Some instruments help people recognize their own understandings and predispositions. Discussing the *Myers-Briggs Type Indicator*® instrument and other personal assessment instruments can help people understand their own views of the world, their patterns for absorbing information and making decisions, and their lifestyles. Numerous other instruments may also contribute to greater individual understanding. The facilitator might want to try many of them and then settle on a couple that best fit the organization's culture and employees.

As they understand themselves through instruments like these, learners often begin to understand others as well. We do not all have the same values, learning styles, motivators, perceptions, or tendencies. This may be the first time some people realize that behavior that is different from their own is the result of different ways of understanding the world.

Current Skills Inventory

Stage for learner: 1, 2, or 3

Context for learning: Semiformal

Learning styles best accommodated: Activist, Pragmatist, Reflector

Outcome of learning: Knowledge, Attitude/Values

Learning resources role: Facilitate process individually or in groups.

People must be aware of their current skills in order to understand the foundation of their future learning. They may be able to identify those skills by examining their past accomplishments.

1. First, ask participants to list up to 10 things they have done that made them feel successful—even if only momentarily—such as writing a research paper, teaching a child to drive, finding a job, coaching a children's sports team, or organizing a project.

2. Next, ask them to select three items from Step 1 that were most important to them.

3. Have the participants write a short narrative for each of these three items describing what they did. They may use a paragraph, list, or outline form—whatever is comfortable for them. (This component may be time-consuming. It could be given as a homework assignment and discussed at a second meeting.)

4. If the skills inventory is being done in small groups, divide into triads (groups of three). Each member of the triad has a role: learner

(A), coach (B), and observer/recorder (C). A describes his or her successes. B listens and questions A to determine the skills A used. C observes the process and records the skills that are identified. When the first round is over, C repeats the skills to A and B to confirm the validity of the record.

5. The exercise has three rounds, so each participant will be able to play each role.

Another method for inventorying current skills is to develop a list of skills that fit into job families, such as verbal, information management, investigative, planning/design, human relations, administrative, and physical. Resources such as *What Color Is Your Parachute?* (Bolles, 1999) may help with this listing. As homework, ask each person to identify which of the listed skills represent strong points and which ones could use some improvement. They should also identify the listed skills they currently lack but would like to acquire. Skills identified in this process become the basis for individual development plans.

Comprehensive Personal Development Workshop

Stage for learner: 1, 2, or 3

Context for learning: Formal, Semiformal

Learning styles best accommodated: Activist, Pragmatist, Reflector

Outcome of learning: Knowledge, Attitude/Values, Skill Development, Aspiration

Learning resources role: Develop workshop, advertise, recruit participants, present workshop or hire presenter, develop follow-up mechanism.

The Personal Development Workshop, which provides some structure and support for learners who are just beginning to learn to learn, is a quasi-formal approach to developing self-awareness. This workshop is similar to a procedure in *What Color Is Your Parachute?* (Bolles, 1999), but it takes place in a group setting, rather than individually, and with a facilitator. For those who have not yet learned to manage their own learning, a workshop may be much more effective than self-management.

The Personal Development Workshop will lead people to think deeply about themselves. They will probably talk about things that they would not want repeated outside the group. A private meeting space is imperative, and, early in the session, the participants should work out a firm understanding of the importance of confidentiality. This discussion will also help establish trust and openness among the participants.

Part 1: Personal Knowledge

In the first half-day session, participants spend time getting to know themselves through their values, learning styles, motivators, and so on. When you create your own personal development workshop, you may not need all the components mentioned, or you may want to add assessment tools with which you are more comfortable. Feel free to substitute your favorites. I recommend a battery of four to six modules to develop a holistic perspective of self.

This part of the workshop might include components such as values clarification, learning lifeline, learning style determination, personal motivators, and perceptions and tendencies. A current skills inventory might be appropriate as homework between Parts 1 and 2 of the workshop.

Part 2: Development Plan

The second half-day session focuses on goals and goal setting. If participants were given homework on current skills, begin with a short discussion to move from skill identification to planning preparation. Once the transition is made, create a framework for individual planning by talking about the organization's direction and what jobs are likely to be available in the future. Participants can then determine if there is alignment between their future and that of the organization.

If there is alignment, participants should write a personal development plan designed around their goals within the organization. If not, the personal development plan may focus on another interesting job. Experience has shown that even when a potential job is outside the organization, employees' current job performance improves because the company has demonstrated commitment to them. Frequently, somewhere during the learning process, the employee decides to continue with the current company rather than move on. If a total mismatch between the

EXERCISE 4: PERSONAL DEVELOPMENT PLAN

PART 1: PERSONAL KNOWLEDGE

My learning style: _____

My most important values: _____

Current key skills: _____

Key skills to be developed: _____

PART 2: DEVELOPMENT PLAN

What is to be learned? _____

How will this be learned? _____

What resources are necessary (time, money, materials, other people)?

_____

How will I know when I have learned what I set out to learn?

_____

What is my target date for completion of this learning?

_____

individual and the direction of the organization exists, the development planning process may guide the participant to a new organization.

Alternatively, the person doing the planning may be perfectly satisfied with work at present and expect that satisfaction to continue for the foreseeable future. In this case, the personal development plan may be non-career related.

When writing a personal development plan, people should list details that are relevant to their values, learning styles, individual preferences, current skills, and so on. As shown above in Exercise 4, the Personal Development Plan should include what will be learned, how it will be learned, what resources will be needed, how success will be determined, and the target date for completion. A form like this one may be developed for ongoing reference.

It is important to remember that taking classes and reading books are not the only ways to learn. Chapters 6 through 11 describe numerous additional learning methods, including the following, which are grouped by the context for the learning.

Formal
Courses
Technical school
College/university
Learning networks

Semiformal
Team development
Mentors
Workshops
Projects
Simulations
Learning networks
Case studies
Distance learning
Computer conferencing
Seminars
Conferences
CD-ROMs
Coaching
Interactive videos
Role play

Nonformal
Visits
Development centers
Shadowing
Internet
Volunteer work
Keeping a journal
Reading
Employee interactions
Networking
Research
Tapes (audio or video)
Dialogue
Job swaps
Presentations
Exploration
Observation
360° Feedback

Individual Personal Development Counseling

Stage for learner: 1, 2, or 3

Context for learning: Nonformal

Learning styles best accommodated: Activist, Pragmatist, Theorist, Reflector

Outcome of learning: Knowledge, Attitude/Values, Skill Development, Aspiration

Learning resources role: Publicize availability of service, arrange for a counselor.

The Personal Development Workshop could be conducted one-on-one, with a facilitator who is familiar with the assessment tools and the development planning process. Activities could be scheduled for two half-day sessions or six to eight weekly one-hour sessions. A theoretical or reflective learner could use the additional time between weekly sessions to give careful consideration to new knowledge or engage in in-depth discussion of the concepts.

Self-Study in Personal Development

Stage for learner: 2 or 3

Context for learning: Nonformal

Learning styles best accommodated: Pragmatist, Theorist, Reflector

Outcome of learning: Knowledge, Attitude/Values, Skill Development, Aspiration

Learning resources role: Write workbook, facilitate development of computer-based modules, publicize opportunity, be available to offer assistance.

A facilitator who is familiar with the personal assessment tools and personal development planning process could assemble the Personal Development Workshop activities into self-study workbooks or create computer modules. A learner could work through the activities independently, with the facilitator available to provide assistance as needed.

Software for Competency Evaluation

Stage for learner: 2 or 3

Context for learning: Semiformal

Learning styles best accommodated: Activist, Pragmatist

Outcome of learning: Knowledge, Aspiration

Learning resources role: Obtain program, orient learners as to its use.

Computer programs are available to assist people in determining their own skills. For example, Knowledge PDP™ from Knowledge Associates provides a Web/intranet-based system for identifying and recording key competencies. Individuals record their current levels of performance as well as the levels to which they aspire. They reflect on experiences and their applicability to these competencies on an ongoing basis.

360° Feedback—Learning How Others Perceive Us

Stage for learner: 3 or 4

Context for learning: Nonformal, Informal

Learning styles best accommodated: Pragmatist, Theorist, Reflector

Outcome of learning: Knowledge, Attitude/Values, Aspiration

Learning resources role: Develop and coordinate process.

Some organizations have incorporated 360° feedback into their human resources development process. Individuals may use this process to learn more about themselves and the way others perceive them. The knowledge then becomes the basis for future learning.

Key elements of using 360° feedback for personal learning are

- It must be voluntary. Coercion makes for a poor learning environment, whereas if the participant requests the feedback, the process will probably be more effective.

- A neutral third party collects feedback unless the learner has used this tool before and openness is part of the organization's culture. At first, the process is smoother with a neutral third party because those providing feedback are more likely to be open and honest. However, after everyone involved has become comfortable with the process, the learner should be able to gather the feedback directly. When this ideal level of openness is reached, development will be greater for everyone.

- If feedback is collected by a third party, that person should simply organize the information and give it to the learner. Giving the information to the learner's supervisor or manager would intimidate and distract the learner and should never be done unless the learner specifically requests it.

- Learners determine what happens to the information. While they should be encouraged to share the newly gathered information with others, they may not feel comfortable about doing so. If a third party gathered the feedback, that individual might act as a learning coach. Although this is a great learning forum, participants often find it difficult to share this kind of information with those who provided the feedback. Therefore, the idea might be suggested but not required.

7

Individual Learning Tools and Strategies for Knowledge and Skills

Behaviors that define learning and those that define being productive are one and the same. Learning is at the heart of productive activity. To put it simply, learning is the new form of labor.

SHOSHANA ZUBROFF
In the Age of the Smart Machine

Peter was the manager of a production facility. He was concerned about his performance and wondered how the supervisors who reported to him perceived him as a leader. He contacted his corporate human resources manager for a tool to help him understand these issues. The manager distributed an anonymous questionnaire to all of Peter's direct reports. He then summarized the data and shared it with Peter.

Peter engaged the services of an external personal coach. They discussed the feedback. After balancing the new information with his own view of his performance and his relationship with his direct reports, Peter defined specific steps for leadership growth and incorporated them into his personal development plan.

The feedback had identified one issue, which was that his direct reports felt he withheld information from them. To show that he was serious about developing the targeted skills, Peter called a meeting with his direct reports and explained what he had learned from the exercise and how he planned to make improvements. An outside facilitator led a discussion to elicit responses from the direct reports regarding Peter's revelations and plans.

As a result of this exercise, several of Peter's direct reports conducted similar self-evaluations. For both Peter and his direct reports, the process was voluntary and was conducted for personal development only.

Introduction to Ongoing Individual Learning

After individuals enter a learning mode, the challenge is to keep them learning on a regular basis. Some learning options may come naturally, but many need to be created and reinforced. As previously mentioned, it is important to have a menu of options for various types of learners. Place flyers with brief descriptions of available options and learning opportunities in the employee break room, with department heads or supervisors, and in the resource center library, if applicable.

Characteristics of Individual Learning Tools

As you go about the selection process, you may decide to offer many different types of learning to accommodate multiple learning styles and to vary the degree of direct relationship to the workplace. Table 5 on pages 118 and 119 lists all the individual learning tools outlined in this chapter and is designed to assist you with your selections.

Learning Tools

The following examples of tools to assist learners may be of use or, alternatively, may assist you in generating additional ideas for tools that better fit your organization.

To-Learn List

Stage for learner: 2, 3, or 4

Context for learning: Informal

Learning styles best accommodated: Activist, Pragmatist, Theorist, Reflector

Outcome of learning: Knowledge, Skill Development

Learning resources role: Provide information about process, create "To-Learn List" for interested learners.

Most of us are familiar with to-do lists. The to-learn list, which details specific learning objectives, is a slight twist (Collins, 1999). As learners gain knowledge about items on the list, they may want to highlight them as a way of marking their accomplishments.

Learning Log or Journal

Stage for learner: 2, 3, or 4

Context for learning: Informal

Learning styles best accommodated: Theorist, Reflector

Outcome of learning: Knowledge, Skill Development

Learning resources role: Provide information about process.

Some people find that keeping a daily journal is an excellent learning mechanism. Participants may use a learning log, which is similar to a journal, to write about what they have learned from a day's events (Collins, 1999). The writings should be kept in a particular book—a bound journal or a simple spiral notebook. People often find that if they establish a specific time each day to write about the day's experiences, they are more likely to keep up with their journals. The learning log serves as a record of a learner's progress; rereading it at a later date often yields surprising realizations of how knowledge grows over time. The log also provides a reference for future development planning.

For those with more verbal learning styles, logs may be used to generate discussion that will further enhance learning. Others may benefit from the conversation as well. Alternatively, prior to writing about any learning event, a participant could discuss it with a peer.

Tape-Recording Self

Stage for learner: 4

Context for learning: Informal

Learning styles best accommodated: Theorist, Reflector

Outcome of learning: Knowledge, Skill Development

Learning resources role: Provide information about process, perhaps provide resources such as tape recorders and tapes.

TABLE 5   ONGOING INDIVIDUAL LEARNING SELECTION

LEARNING MODE	Stage for Learner	Context for Learning	Complementary Learning Style(s)	Outcome of Learning	Work Related?
To-Learn List	2, 3, 4	Informal	Activist, Pragmatist, Theorist, Reflector	Knowledge, Skill	Possibly
Learning Log or Journal	2, 3, 4	Informal	Theorist, Reflector	Knowledge, Skill	Yes
Tape-Recording Self	4	Informal	Theorist, Reflector	Knowledge, Skill	Yes
Job Shadowing	1, 2, 3, 4	Nonformal, Informal	Activist, Pragmatist, Reflector	Knowledge, Aspiration	Yes
Observation of Unfamiliar Meeting	1, 2, 3, 4	Semiformal	Activist, Pragmatist, Reflector	Knowledge, Aspiration	Yes
Temporary Job Swaps	3, 4	Nonformal	Activist, Pragmatist, Theorist, Reflector	Knowledge, Skill	Yes
Direct Customer Contact	1, 2, 3	Nonformal	Activist, Pragmatist	Knowledge, Skill	Yes
Reading and Reflecting	2, 3, 4	Nonformal, Informal	Theorist, Reflector	Knowledge, Attitude/Values	Possibly
Reflecting on Audio- or Videotapes	1, 2, 3	Nonformal	Pragmatist, Reflector	Knowledge, Skill	Yes
Self-Study Workbook Programs	2, 3	Nonformal	Activist, Pragmatist, Reflector	Knowledge, Skill, Attitude/Values	Yes

Activity	Levels	Formality	Learning Styles	Knowledge/Skill	Recommended
Individual Research Projects–from Diagnosis to Evaluation	3, 4	Nonformal	Activist, Pragmatist, Theorist, Reflector	Knowledge, Skill	Yes
Learning Through Innovation–Encouraging Creativity	3, 4	Nonformal	Activist, Pragmatist, Theorist, Reflector	Knowledge, Skill	Yes
Public Speaking and Presentations	2, 3, 4	Informal, Semiformal	Activist, Pragmatist, Reflector	Knowledge, Skill	Possibly
Volunteer Work and Community Service	2, 3, 4	Informal	Activist, Pragmatist, Theorist, Reflector	Knowledge, Skill Attitude/Values, Aspiration	Possibly
Adapting Workshops and Seminars to Individual Learning Styles	1, 2, 3, 4	Formal, Semiformal	Activist, Pragmatist Theorist, Reflector	Knowledge, Skill	Yes
Memberships for Networking, Interactive Learning	2, 3, 4	Nonformal	Activist, Pragmatist	Knowledge, Skill	Yes
Video Teleconferencing for Interactive Distance Learning	2, 3, 4	Formal	Pragmatist, Theorist, Reflector	Knowledge, Skill	Yes
Internet Study for College Credit	2, 3, 4	Semiformal	Activist, Pragmatist, Reflector	Knowledge, Skill	Yes
Computer-Based Modules for Training	2, 3	Nonformal	Activist, Pragmatist, Reflector	Knowledge, Skill	Yes
Knowledge PDP™–Software to Track Performance	2, 3, 4	Semiformal	Activist, Pragmatist, Reflector	Knowledge	Yes

Instead of writing in a learning log, participants could tape-record themselves—in meetings or during other interactions. Later, when they play back the tapes, they should be alert for indications of how others may be hearing them as well as for additional clues to their learning needs and development. If the learner spends a good deal of time in the car, he or she may choose to listen while driving. In this case, a hand-held tape recorder might be useful to capture observations and insights.

Learners who tape themselves require a high level of self-discipline, especially if they are listening to often lengthy meetings or other events in which they have already participated. This option also demands a certain level of discretion. Other participants could be concerned about why they are being taped. The learner may want to diplomatically assure them that the taping is for self-development purposes and will not be shared with anyone else.

Job Shadowing

Stage for learner: 1, 2, 3, or 4

Context for learning: Nonformal, Informal

Learning styles best accommodated: Activist, Pragmatist, Reflector

Outcome of learning: Knowledge, Aspiration

Learning resources role: Provide information about program, facilitate matching learners at Stages 1 or 2 (Stage 3 or 4 learners can usually facilitate own match), provide reflection form.

Job shadowing is a valuable learning tool. It can be used to broaden an employee's understanding of his or her own work and its impact on others or to explore another career.

In the first instance, the learner shadows another person in the company, perhaps an internal customer (someone who uses the learner's products or services) or an internal supplier (someone who provides raw materials or services to the learner). The learner acquires a better idea of both jobs and how they affect each other.

Alternatively, job shadowing could be part of a career exploration. The learner spends time with a person who is doing the kind of work in which he or she is interested. This process provides a firsthand look at

Name: _____ Date: _____

Job/Person shadowed: _____

1. What are the main things I have learned from this experience?

2. What will I do differently as a result of this experience?

3. What additional things has this experience stimulated me to learn about? When will I learn them? How?

Figure 6   Employee Interaction Reflection Form

the realities of the job and could lead to a mentoring relationship that includes regular meetings.

Job shadowing is generally a half- to full-day experience.

The facilitator should provide a form, such as the one in Figure 6, to help learners articulate what they have learned.

Observation of Unfamiliar Meeting

Stage for learner: 1, 2, 3, or 4

Context for learning: Semiformal

Learning styles best accommodated: Theorist, Reflector

Outcome of learning: Knowledge, Aspiration

Learning resources role: Provide information about opportunities, coordinate individual attendance at meeting, provide reflection form.

Sometimes simply observing a meeting can be a learning experience. The meeting may occur at an organizational level or in a department other than the learner's, or it could be within the same department but pertain to an unfamiliar topic or project. For instance, a production worker might sit in on a meeting for a production management group or a cross-functional project team.

Afterward, a supervisor or learning resources person should conduct a debriefing. Alternatively, provide an Observation Reflection Form, similar to the Employee Interaction Reflection Form in Figure 6, to help the learner assess the experience.

Temporary Job Swaps

Stage for learner: 3 or 4

Context for learning: Nonformal

Learning styles best accommodated: Activist, Pragmatist, Theorist, Reflector

Outcome of learning: Knowledge, Skill Development

Learning resources role: Coordinate with sites involved, work with sites or committee in selecting participants and mentors, orient mentors, schedule for debriefing session with everyone at the end.

As part of a leadership development program, some organizations have instituted job swaps. These are temporary reassignments for specific lengths of time, usually six months to a year.

Schedule regular one-hour debriefings at which participants may discuss what they are learning from the job-swap experience. You might want to involve a learning coach to facilitate the sessions.

Guarantee in writing that the learner can return to his or her original job, and add a clause stating that inability to perform in the temporary job is not grounds for termination. It would also be prudent to specify that, in the latter case, the learner could return to his or her permanent position or occupy an equivalent one for the duration of the job-swap term.

Direct Customer Contact

Stage for learner: 1, 2, or 3

Context for learning: Nonformal

Learning styles best accommodated: Activist, Pragmatist

Outcome of learning: Knowledge, Skill Development

Learning resources role: Provide information about opportunity, coordinate with customer service, provide access to writing or telephone skills development opportunities if required.

Working with the customer service department provides opportunities for direct customer contact. Have the learner spend one hour per week

Name: _____   Date: _____

Book/article read: _____

Author: _____

1. What are the main points the author is trying to convey in this book, article, or chapter?

2. What are the main things I learned from this book, article, or chapter?

3. What additional things do I want to learn as a result of reading this book, article, or chapter?

Figure 7   Reading Reflection Form

working with a customer service person on matters relating to that department. If you have a retail operation, the learner could spend some time there, such as an hour each week or half a day every month. Provide a reflection form similar to the one in Figure 6 to help the employee clarify what he or she learned during each session.

Reading and Reflecting

Stage for learner: 2, 3, or 4

Context for learning: Nonformal, Informal

Learning styles best accommodated: Theorist, Reflector

Outcome of learning: Knowledge, Attitude/Values

Learning resources role: Provide information about books and articles, provide reflection form.

Reading about topics of interest can be an effective form of learning for those whose primary or secondary learning style is reading. To make the effort more effective, you might provide a simple reading reflection form such as the one in Figure 7 above.

To further expand the value of the reading process, form a group to discuss common readings.

Reflecting on Audio- or Videotapes

Stage for learner: 1, 2, or 3

Context for learning: Nonformal

Learning styles best accommodated: Pragmatist, Reflector

Outcome of learning: Knowledge, Skill Development

Learning resources role: Provide information about available audio- and videotapes, act as librarian to keep track of tapes, provide reflection form.

For those whose primary or secondary learning style is auditory, listening to audiotapes or viewing videotapes may be an effective learning strategy. Again, a form similar to the Reading Reflection Form in Figure 7 may assist the participant in deepening his or her level of learning. You may also want to consider forming a group to discuss audio- or videotapes.

Self-Study Workbook Programs

Stage for learner: 2 or 3

Context for learning: Nonformal

Learning styles best accommodated: Activist, Pragmatist, Reflector

Outcome of learning: Knowledge, Skill Development, Attitude/Values

Learning resources role: Identify critical areas for learning in the organization, obtain or create modules, provide information about program, act as librarian to keep track of resources.

Self-study workbooks may be effective learning tools for those who can remain on task. Workbooks address a range of topics, from basic maintenance to computer use to interpersonal skills. The Crisp Publications series provides introductory self-study in several "soft skills" areas. Some organizations have written their own self-study programs, tailored to their specific needs. A Quick Learning Resources series developed by an engineering-oriented company provides a case in point.

Quick Learning Resources

The learning resources staff at a large engineering-oriented firm created a series of workbooks that have become career enhancers for many employees. Quick Learning Resources are short, self-managed courses in soft skills. Each component is less than three hours in length. Quick Learning Resources are housed in the company's career center and may be checked out by any company employee. Topics include

- Career strategies: career self-analysis, career and lifestyle planning, trends in the business world

- Communications and interpersonal skills: general communications; receiving and giving feedback; listening skills; male/female communications; meetings; negotiation; people relationships, enhancement and conflicts; public speaking; telephone communications; vocabulary building; written communications

- Creativity and models

- Customer service and relations

- Job hunting strategies and resources: entrepreneurship, interviewing, job descriptions, job search strategies, job sources, negotiating salaries, networking, retirement, writing résumés and cover letters

- Leadership and management development: coaching for top performance; hiring; leadership development; management skills, executive and supervisory; management trends and overviews; coping with change and stress

- *Myers-Briggs Type Indicator*® types and Keirsey temperaments

- Personal improvement: achievement and success; change, transitions, and risk taking; goal and priority setting; health, emotional and physical; humor; learning and memory techniques; mentoring; money management; motivation and psychological improvement; organizing skills; stress management; time management

- Project management

- Secretarial skills

- Teams

- Total quality

- Women, men, and diversity

Individual Research Projects—from Diagnosis to Evaluation

Stage for learner: 3 or 4

Context for learning: Nonformal

Learning styles best accommodated: Activist, Pragmatist, Theorist, Reflector

Outcome of learning: Knowledge, Skill Development

Learning resources role: Assist learners in developing a project or put learners in contact with someone who can help develop it; assist in developing the system, if it is to be institutionalized.

A research project is a planned, focused effort to acquire a specific knowledge or skill. The topic can be of personal interest or work related. The process includes

- Diagnosing a learning need

- Formulating learning goals

- Identifying resources—people, time, money

- Choosing and implementing learning strategies

- Evaluating what has been learned

Learning Through Innovation—Encouraging Creativity

Stage for learner: 3 or 4

Context for learning: Nonformal

Learning styles best accommodated: Activist, Pragmatist, Theorist, Reflector

Outcome of learning: Knowledge, Skill Development

Learning resources role: Assist in developing system, procure learning materials as needed.

An organization that is interested in innovation should develop mechanisms to support it. A policy instituted by 3M allows employees in technical positions to spend up to 15% of their time working on innovative ideas of their own selection (Brand, 1998). In the next phase, the Genesis grant program enables technical workers to buy equipment that will assist them in developing their ideas. Alternatively, the grants pay for temporary workers to fill in for the learners while they are developing their ideas (Brand, 1998). Alpha grants fund development of new ideas or processes in areas outside the technical units.

Public Speaking and Presentations

Stage for learner: 2, 3, or 4

Context for learning: Informal, Semiformal (speaking club)

Learning styles best accommodated: Activist, Pragmatist, Reflector

Outcome of learning: Knowledge, Skill Development

Learning resources role: Provide information on opportunities, locate places to speak or set up a speaking club.

Most people claim public speaking as one of their worst fears. Perhaps the best way to conquer the fear is to face it—by speaking publicly. Making successful public presentations takes practice. Learners should select a topic they know well or learn about a new one that may be interesting to others and offer to speak on it. Service clubs are often looking for people to speak on interesting new topics.

Another option is to create an in-house speaking club. The Toastmasters format provides a structured model for learning to speak in front of others who share an interest in public speaking and who are just learning as well—which should make the process a little less intimidating.

Volunteer Work and Community Service

Stage for learner: 2, 3, or 4

Context for learning: Informal

Learning styles best accommodated: Activist, Pragmatist, Theorist, Reflector

Outcome of learning: Knowledge, Skill Development, Attitude/Values, Aspiration

Learning resources role: Assist learner in identifying appropriate organization; for in-house project, facilitate design and implementation of program, perhaps by forming a committee of volunteers.

Volunteer work can be a terrific learning opportunity that also benefits the community. It can relate to business in general or to your workplace specifically. For instance, Junior Achievement provides opportunities for teaching the basics of economics to schoolchildren of different age groups. In teaching others, volunteers learn about the economic system and the process of helping others learn. Begin at the elementary school level and work up.

Habitat for Humanity offers the chance to learn practical skills like house building and renovating. An employee who serves on the board of directors for a nonprofit organization may learn and practice new management skills. Another option is to join a committee or sit on the board of directors of the local chamber of commerce. Learners could become involved in arts, educational, religious, environmental, health, human services, or other groups that benefit society.

Through volunteer work, people acquire the skills of problem solving, decision making, budgeting, and interpersonal relations. As learners maintain their involvement with a specific organization, their education will likely progress from simple tasks to complex decision making.

Adapting Workshops and Seminars to Individual Learning Styles

Stage for learner: 1, 2, 3, or 4

Context for learning: Formal, Semiformal

Learning styles best accommodated: Activist, Pragmatist, Theorist, Reflector

Outcome of learning: Knowledge, Skill Development

Learning resources role: Assist learner to think through learning need, to identify potential learning programs, and examine the pros and cons of selected programs.

Workshops or seminars on a topic of interest represent a more traditional approach to learning. If the topic fits a specific development need and participants are open to this kind of learning, it can be effective. Even if classroom or lecture settings do not fit the learners' particular styles, they may still benefit from attending the workshop or seminar. The challenge will be to adapt it to their learning style. For instance, visual learners may want to do some reading about the topic in advance, or auditory learners may want to lead a post-session discussion group on the topic to verbally process what they have learned.

Memberships for Networking, Interactive Learning

Stage for learner: 2, 3, or 4

Context for learning: Nonformal

Learning styles best accommodated: Activist, Pragmatist

Outcome of learning: Knowledge, Skill Development

Learning resources role: Assist learner to think through learning need, to identify potential organizations to join, and to examine pros and cons of the selected organization.

Membership in organizations and attendance at conferences and conventions provide access to learning opportunities and the chance to network with others of similar interests. Most organizations conduct workshops and publish newsletters and trade journals exclusively for their members. A local unit often provides convenient access for a more hands-on, interactive learning approach. As with serving on voluntary boards of directors, longer involvment leads to a higher level of learning.

Video Teleconferencing for Interactive Distance Learning

Stage for learner: 2, 3, or 4

Context for learning: Formal

Learning styles best accommodated: Pragmatist, Theorist, Reflector

Outcome of learning: Knowledge, Skill Development

Learning resources role: Provide information about available opportunities, coordinate development with external educational institutions, arrange for technical equipment.

Some organizations are taking advantage of distance learning programs through video teleconferencing. For example, Los Alamos National Laboratory is located in a remote setting, and employees do not have access to institutions. In 1984, the laboratory initiated distance learning by establishing an electronic hook-up with the University of New Mexico to enable employees to earn college degrees. Course lectures are telecast into the Los Alamos classrooms. Microphones allow questions and interactive communication. A courier shuttles between the two sites once a week to transport handouts and assignments. Since its inception, the program has awarded 96 bachelor's degrees, 142 master's degrees, and 4 doctorates.

Your organization could make similar arrangements. This could be especially valuable if you are located in an isolated area.

Internet Study for College Credit

Stage for learner: 2, 3, or 4

Context for learning: Semiformal

Learning styles best accommodated: Activist, Pragmatist, Reflector

Outcome of learning: Knowledge, Skill Development

Learning resources role: Provide information about available opportunities, arrange for technical equipment; if necessary, coordinate development with external educational institutions.

Many colleges, universities, and other institutions offer college-credit classes on the Internet. Often, classes allow lessons, exercises, and collaborative work to be done online. This approach requires no infrastructure investment from the organization. As long as participants have Internet access and know use a search engine, they can learn online. Be sure to confirm the viability of the institution and the quality of the classes. Some have simply taken a classroom format and brought it online. Others have developed the online course into a true learning experience. To deal with the question of quality, some organizations specifiy that company money can only be spent for tuition if the online provider is accredited by recognized institutions.

Computer-Based Modules for Training

Stage for learner: 2 or 3

Context for learning: Nonformal

Learning styles best accommodated: Activist, Pragmatist, Reflector

Outcome of learning: Knowledge, Skill Development

Learning resources role: Provide information about available opportunities, arrange for development of modules and technical equipment.

Many companies have developed computer-based training that may be downloaded directly onto an employee's workplace computer. Motorola delivers one of its required courses by CD-ROM (Galagan, 1994). In a program called Employee Knowledge Link, Pacific Bell uses a digital network to deliver training materials to workstations (Galagan, 1994). These programs include text, graphics, photographs, audio, and video. They may be purchased from software suppliers or developed in-house by information technology staff in conjunction with training and/or human resources development personnel.

Knowledge PDP™–Software to Track Performance

Stage for learner: 2, 3, or 4

Context for learning: Semiformal

Learning styles best accommodated: Activist, Pragmatist, Reflector

Outcome of learning: Knowledge

Learning resources role: Obtain software, instruct learners in its use.

Knowledge PDP™ is an intranet-based program that helps identify key competencies (Knowledge PDP, 1999). It allows individuals to track their current performance levels and aspirations by creating a database of their daily activities, learning experiences, and new skills.

8

Mentoring, Coaching, and Peer Learning Approaches

Self-education is, I believe, the only kind of learning there is.

ISAAC ASIMOV

A manufacturing company was looking for a member development coordinator to lead its learning system. After an extensive search, they had not found anyone who both understood the concept of the learning system and could fit into the company's highly participative culture.

The hiring team decided to hire a person who worked in the plant— a production-line team leader who aspired to a position such as this. He had been developing himself for the role independently for more than a year. He knew the company culture. He understood the role itself, but did not have applicable skills and experience in the job. The team decided to hire him and retain an external personal coach for him as well.

The two met at least once a month for the better part of a day to work on development issues that pertained to the employee's new position. The personal coach asked questions, sometimes challenged plans, and occasionally offered alternatives ideas. In some cases, she facilitated contact with the right resources. At the beginning of the relationship, the coach suggested that the mentoring process would be complete when the new coordinator was providing the coach with information rather than the other way around. At the end of a year, they reached this point, and the relationship was dissolved.

Introduction to One-on-One Learning

Learners often find themselves with the opportunity to learn with and through another person. How can someone focus on individual learning while working with another person? How might dyads promote conscious learning?

Malcolm Knowles (1980) identifies the concept of learner-centered learning—which consists of learners diagnosing their own learning needs, formulating learning objectives, designing learning experiences, and evaluating their own results. In Knowles's design, learners are seen as peers of mentors. Learning takes place through the interaction of the learner and the mentor—they co-create learning.

Characteristics of Peer Learning

As you go about the selection process, you may decide to offer multiple types of learning to accommodate different learning styles and to vary the degree of direct relationship to the workplace. Table 6 lists all the peer learning opportunities described in this chapter and is designed to assist you with your selections.

Learning Tools

The following examples of one-on-one learning may be of use in your learning system, or may assist you in generating new ideas that will better fit your organization.

Mentoring Programs—Why, How, for Whom

Stage for learner: 3 or 4

Context for learning: Nonformal

Learning styles best accommodated: Theorist, Reflector

Outcome of learning: Knowledge, Skill Development, Attitude/Values, Aspiration

Learning resources role: Facilitate creation of process, publicize, coordinate, follow up with mentoring pairs.

TABLE 6   PEER LEARNING SELECTION

	Stage for Learner	Context for Learning	Complementary Learning Style(s)	Outcome of Learning	Work Related?
ONE-ON-ONE LEARNING RELATIONSHIPS					
Mentoring Programs—Why, How, for Whom	3, 4	Nonformal	Theorist, Reflector	Knowledge, Skill, Attitude/Values, Aspirations	Yes
Informational Interviews	2, 3	Nonformal	Activist, Pragmatist, Reflector	Knowledge, Skill, Aspiration	Yes
Coaching for Learning Skills	2, 3	Semiformal, Nonformal	Activist, Pragmatist	Knowledge, Skill	Yes
Personal Coach Contracted from Outside the Company	3	Nonformal	Pragmatist, Theorist, Reflector	Knowledge, Skill, Attitude/Values	Yes
Strategic Development Advisers for Specific Areas	2, 3	Nonformal	Activist, Pragmatist, Theorist, Reflector	Knowledge, Skill	Yes
Peer Coaching for Specific Skills	1, 2	Nonformal	Activist, Pragmatist	Knowledge, Skill, Attitude/Values	Yes
Peer Tutoring for Learning a Language	1, 2	Formal, Nonformal	Activist, Pragmatist	Knowledge, Skill	Yes
Technical Peer Mentoring for New Employees	1	Semiformal	Activist, Pragmatist, Theorist, Reflector	Knowledge, Skill, Attitude/Values	Yes
Foreign-Language Peer Tutoring	2, 3	Nonformal	Activist, Pragmatist	Knowledge, Skill	Possibly
Peer Dyads	3, 4	Noniformal	Theorist, Reflector	Knowledge, Skill, Attitude/Values	Yes

Taken literally, *mentor* may be defined as a trusted adviser. Mentoring relationships sometimes form when potential mentors meet learners who interest them. The mentor then seeks to develop the learner or protégé, over a period of time through informal or semiformal meetings. Alternatively, mentoring relationships may occur when a learner finds a person who is knowledgeable in an area of interest. In that case, the protégé initiates the relationship. When organizations have a strong desire to use mentoring, but these relationships have not formed naturally on a widespread basis, mentoring programs provide a means of formalizing the process.

A mentoring relationship requires mutual trust and develops over time. In Phase 1, the entry phase, the mentor and protégé get to know each other as individuals while discussing areas of mutual interest. During Phase 2, mutual trust develops as they work together, learn from each other, and enjoy reciprocal reliability and support. Mutual risk taking begins to occur during Phase 3, when the mentor encourages the learner to stretch. Not all attempts will result in success, but even the failures represent opportunities for mutual learning. In Phase 4, the mentor and learner understand each other and create new learning together. In Phase 5, the learner internalizes the process of learning to learn and initiates changes in the mentoring relationship. In Phase 6, the learner assumes the lead role and the mentor is in a less dominant position—the learner begins either to separate from the mentor or to become a colleague on equal footing.

The major components of a mentoring program include

1. Identification of a coordinator

2. Identification of potential protégés

3. Identification of potential mentors

4. Development and implementation of an information/orientation session on the mentoring process for both mentors and protégés

5. Creation of a process for aligning mentors and protégés

6. Follow-up with mentoring pairs to ensure a good fit

Lindenberger and Zachary (1999) were involved in a mentoring program at Brown-Forman Corporation. They describe the requirements for implementing the program in the following way:

- The process should be voluntary; self-initiated pairings of mentors and protégés work best. Information shared between the two should be confidential.

- Allocate time for learning about mentoring.

- Develop simple mentor and protégé biography sheets so that each member of the prospective pair may learn about the other's career and personal background.

- The program should support informal mentoring that is already in progress.

- Determine clear learning outcomes for the relationship early in the association.

- Face-to-face, telephone, or e-mail meetings should take place between mentor and protégé at least once a month, and at least one of the mentoring sessions should occur off-site.

- Publicize the program by a variety of means including newsletter articles, corporate leadership speeches, and quarterly meetings on the topic.

- Involve people throughout the organization in the creation and ongoing activities of the mentoring program. Enlist advocates to champion the program.

- Information on the mentoring program should be available at the resource center.

- Assess the value of the program through confidential exit interviews of both parties at the end of the formal mentoring relationship.

You may expand the mentoring program by encouraging employees to create their own personal board of directors composed of potential mentors from specific areas throughout the organization (Lindenberger and Zachary, 1999).

Types of Mentoring Programs

An engineering-based firm offers a number of different mentoring programs, which are all overseen by the career development coordinator.

Mentoring programs include

- New hire/new graduate mentoring

- Cross-cultural mentoring (for mid-career women and minorities)

- Technical group supervisors mentoring (for first-level managers)

- Project element managers and task managers mentoring (for first-level project management)

- Secretarial mentoring

- Step-two career coaching (employee meets with a manager two levels above for career discussion)

Because there are so many different mentoring programs, the engineering company pairs mentors and protégés through a variety of procedures.

In the *new hire/new graduate program,* each division has a mentoring representative. Representatives ask new hires if they would like to participate in the mentoring program. If they say yes, the representative selects a mentor from a volunteer pool. A mentor must not have a direct reporting relationship with the learner or be in a position that provides input to the learner's performance evaluation. Each mentor gets a half day of training in the process of initiating and developing the mentoring relationship.

The *cross-cultural mentoring program* lasts for one year. It is advertised through the organization's newsletter and e-mail. Information about the program and an application form are available on the company's intranet Web page. There are a total of 18 slots divided among the company's divisions. When an employee applies for the program, the application is submitted to the career development coordinator. The coordinator then forwards the application to a divisional mentoring representative, who takes them to a division manager, who selects the final candidates. If a division refuses a slot, it is given to a different division. Those with the most candidates are given priority. Since this is a mid-career program for minorities and women, protégés are matched with mentors from divisions other than their own to ensure development of a broader organizational perspective. Additionally, cross-division matching makes the protégés more visible, which is one of the goals of the program. Representatives present their candidate(s) at a meeting of all division representatives, who may suggest potential mentors. The representatives then match mentors with learners. The career development staff provides training and determines the criteria for measuring success. The career development coordinator is also responsible for arranging ongoing activities and following up on the pairings.

Technical group supervisor protégés apply for the mentoring program after taking a group supervisor class, which is part of their ongoing training. Potential mentors are recommended to the technical division mentoring representative by departmental managers. The technical division mentoring representative is responsible for coordinating the mentor-protégé pairings. Since the mentoring program is individualized, it may begin at any time. After the process is under way, responsibility for the ongoing tracking of the program transfers from the technical division mentoring representative to the company's career development coordinator.

The *project element managers and task managers mentoring program* pairs first-level project managers with more experienced ones. The *step-two career coaching* program is broader in scope. An employee meets with a manager two levels up in the organization to discuss longer-term career goals and to devise strategies for attaining the required skills and knowledge.

The *secretarial program* is group oriented and consists of mentoring circles of up to five people. The mentors, an administrative assistant and a senior secretary, hold meetings on the first Tuesday of each month during lunch hour. Several mentoring circles can exist at any time.

The company also encourages informal mentoring relationships. For those who are interested, a mentoring guide is listed on the company intranet.

Dissolving a Mentoring Relationship

In a formal program, it is advisable to establish a time frame for dissolving the mentoring relationship. For instance, there could be a written agreement that the relationship will last for a year. Either party could opt out within the year, or they could agree to continue the relationship on an informal basis. Informal mentoring relationships are less likely to be time based, although at some point, both parties may decide to transform the association into a more collegial one.

Informational Interviews

Stage for learner: 2 or 3

Context for learning: Nonformal

Learning styles best accommodated: Activist, Pragmatist, Reflector

Outcome of learning: Knowledge, Skill Development, Aspiration

Learning resources role: Publicize opportunity, assist learner in identifying potential interviewees.

Informational interviews are a form of short-term mentoring. Learners create a list of people who are either in a more advanced position in a similar function or in an unfamiliar part of the organization. Weekly or monthly, the learner could conduct an informational interview to ask questions such as

- What is your job?

- How does it fit into the organization as a whole?

- What level of education do you have?

- How did you get into the position?

- What is your view of the company's future?

The learner has one meeting with each person on the list. Through this process, the learner will probably learn a great deal about the organization, the individuals, and the requirements for various careers. A long-term mentor may be discovered during the process.

Coaching for Learning Skills

Stage for learner: 2 or 3

Context for learning: Semiformal, Nonformal

Learning styles best accommodated: Activist, Pragmatist

Outcome of learning: Knowledge, Skill Development

Learning resources role: Assist managers and supervisors in becoming coaches.

Coaching and mentoring are often mistaken for the same activity, but there are many key differences between the two (Cunningham, Bennett, and Dawes, 2000). Tactical skills are often the focus of a coach, who is likely to be the learner's boss, in contrast to the emphasis on strategy that distinguishes many mentoring relationships. Coaching may occur only once to teach a specific skill, or it may be done indirectly, when the coach writes up the process of learning a new skill and posts it on the organization's intranet or in a manual in a learning resource center.

Coaching and traditional supervision utilize different sets of skills. Coaching skills may be developed on the job or acquired more formally through a workshop. Chapter 11 outlines a format for a coaching skills workshop. These skills may also be learned through an outside seminar or training program. Learners must select the program carefully to ensure that the focus is truly on people development and is not supervisory management under a new name.

Personal Coach Contracted from Outside the Company

Stage for learner: 3

Context for learning: Nonformal

Learning styles best accommodated: Pragmatist, Theorist, Reflector

Outcome of learning: Knowledge, Skill Development, Attitude/Values

Learning resources role: Create a niche for personal coaches, assist in procuring a personal coach.

Personal coaches assist with individual development, much like mentors, but are usually contracted for a specified time period from outside the company. A variation on executive coaching, personal coaching is designed for those in nonexecutive positions.

Organizations are often faced with the difficult task of finding a person with the requisite skills for a key position who also fits into the culture. Hiring committees sometimes fear promoting a current employee who does not yet have the capabilities to satisfy all of the job requirements. A personal coach may be able to bring an individual into a position and continue to consciously develop the employee over time.

Strategic Development Advisers for Specific Areas

Stage for learner: 2 or 3

Context for learning: Nonformal

Learning styles best accommodated: Activist, Pragmatist, Theorist, Reflector

Outcome of learning: Knowledge, Skill Development

Learning resources role: Develop and coordinate program, orient and support strategic development advisers.

Strategic development advisers are closely related to personal coaches. The term refers to individuals who work one-on-one with learners to help them focus on a specific business area, such as establishing mentor relationships or linking learners to other resources (Cunningham, Bennett, and Dawes, 2000). There may be one strategic development adviser in each business unit of the organization. This person would not report to the human resources staff but would be responsible to his or her own unit. Strategic development advisers from throughout the organization may form a separate informal unit that meets on a regular basis to share experiences and new ideas.

This relationship is not as deep as mentor-protégé or personal coach relationships. It is of a more facilitative nature, as the adviser is likely to work with several learners at the same time.

Peer Coaching for Specific Skills

Stage for learner: 1 or 2

Context for learning: Nonformal

Learning styles best accommodated: Activist, Pragmatist

Outcome of learning: Knowledge, Skill Development, Attitude/Values

Learning resources role: Develop program in conjunction with units desiring the program.

Peer coaching is a form of coaching—the learner wants to acquire specific knowledge or a skill from the coach. Peer coaching may be used to orient new employees or upgrade on-the-job knowledge or skills. Peer coaches should augment their own coaching skills before they agree to help build the skills of others. A train-the-trainer program or coaching workshop should be available to ensure their effectiveness in the coaching role.

Peer Tutoring for Learning a Language

> **Stage for learner:** 1 or 2
>
> **Context for learning:** Formal, Nonformal
>
> **Learning styles best accommodated:** Activist, Pragmatist
>
> **Outcome of learning:** Knowledge, Skill Development
>
> **Learning resources role:** Develop and coordinate program; recruit, orient, and train peer tutors.

Peer tutoring combines classroom training and individual coaching (Gordon, Morgan, and Ponticell, 1995) and is often used to teach English as a second language (and foreign languages; see page 144). The process begins with an assessment of individual needs to determine the learner's English proficiency. The assessment identifies gaps in the level of language proficiency necessary to do the job and specifies criteria for individual success. The classroom instructor determines the sequence of individualized goals for learning English as a second language. In the 40-hour program Gordon and colleagues describe, there are 2 hours of classroom time and 2 hours of tutoring each week for ten weeks. Instructors find that a breakthrough generally occurs after about 15 hours of instruction. Peers are recruited and trained to tutor the students. These volunteers find that they learn a great deal as well. The peer tutoring format could be applied to other necessary skill areas as well.

Technical Peer Mentoring for New Employees

> **Stage for learner:** 1
>
> **Context for learning:** Semiformal
>
> **Learning styles best accommodated:** Activist, Pragmatist, Theorist, Reflector
>
> **Outcome of learning:** Knowledge, Skill Development, Attitude/Values
>
> **Learning resources role:** Develop program in conjunction with units desiring the program.

Microsoft uses peers as mentors for new recruits in technical jobs (Wallace, 1999). The company begins by identifying people who already have the technical knowledge and are willing to become peer mentors. The new employee's manager and the peer mentor meet first to make sure they agree about the new employee's learning needs. Then they inform the new employee of their assessment.

The peer mentors meet with learners for approximately 30 minutes a day for the first few weeks on the job and prioritize what must be learned and in what sequence. They regularly ask open-ended questions to make sure the new employees really understand what they are learning. Learners and their supervisors receive written status reports from peer mentors on a regular basis.

Foreign Language Peer Tutoring

Stage for learner: 2 or 3

Context for learning: Nonformal

Learning styles best accommodated: Activist, Pragmatist

Outcome of learning: Knowledge, Skill Development

Learning resources role: Locate tutors, establish tutoring relationships, follow up to ensure pairs are functioning well.

Foreign languages may be difficult to learn but are often necessary for communicating with coworkers or staff at foreign subsidiaries. Formal classroom instruction is not always the most effective way to teach a foreign language. Oscar Meyer Company came up with a process they call "Each One Teach One" (Manly, Brost, and Houtman, 1997), in which personal development staff introduce an employee who wants to learn a language to a peer tutor who speaks it fluently. The partners decide on their own meeting times and work together on an informal basis.

Peer Dyads

Stage for learner: 3 or 4

Context for learning: Nonformal

Learning styles best accommodated: Theorist, Reflector

Outcome of learning: Knowledge, Skill Development, Attitude/Values

Learning resources role: Facilitate matching dyads.

Learning in twosomes does not always mean that one of the learners is more knowledgeable than the other. Peers can learn from each other if they make a conscious effort. Each member of the dyad should have a specific development plan or skill in mind. For the greatest impact, peers should meet weekly for at least an hour. Each one should report on relevant items such as progress to date, obstacles encountered, and who has been contacted for assistance. Partners can take turns helping each other think through alternative approaches and resources. As the relationship develops and the peers become attuned to each other's development, the rate of learning grows exponentially.

9

Tools and Strategies for Individual Learning in Groups

One may learn by doing the thing; for though you think
you know it, you may have no certainty until you try.

SOPHOCLES
Trachiniae

Springfield Remanufacturing Corporation has a program for third-graders in local schools that is designed to help children understand what business is about (Honold, 1999). The class visits the company, and people who perform different jobs, from forklift driver to business manager, describe their work to the students. At the end of the field trip, the students participate in mock job interviews with employees in jobs of interest to them.

To demonstrate some basic business principles, the company packages sets containing a pen, a pencil, and a ruler. Each student gets 10 kits to sell for $1.50 each. Employees involved in the project help the children record the costs of raw materials and production and the income generated from their sales—a simplified profit-and-loss statement. The profit, if any, is distributed to the children at the end of the project.

In addition to teaching third-graders about business, the employees are also learning. For example, employees have to understand finances well before they can teach it to the children. They cannot teach what they do not understand. It forces them to learn. Company officials believe that involvement with the schools has had a positive impact on employees' self-esteem.

Introduction to Individual Learning in Groups

Individual learning can occur in groups or in teams. As with other approaches, the key is to focus consciously on the learning. Some of the suggestions included in this chapter, such as classes in English as a second language, are based on a more traditional training approach, but with a slight twist. Others, such as learning sets (Cunningham, 1999), reflective note taking (Castleberg, 1999), reading groups, business plan development, and customer champions, are semiformal or nonformal in nature. We will begin with the more formal programs.

Characteristics of Individual Learning in Groups

As you go about the selection process for your learning system, you may decide to offer many different types of learning opportunities to accommodate multiple learning styles and to vary the degree of direct relationship to the workplace. Table 7 on pages 150 and 151 lists all the tools for individual learning in groups discussed in this chapter and is designed to assist you with your selections.

Nontraditional Presentations of Traditional Courses

There may some value in offering classes that employees have already taken if you try to approach the information in a different way. Presented in a format that makes learners feel comfortable, previously difficult subjects may be easier to understand.

Learning Tools

The following examples of tools and strategies for individual learning in groups may be of use in your learning system, or may provide ideas upon which you can build learning opportunities that better fit your organization.

Economics 101

Stage for learner: 1, 2, or 3

Context for learning: Formal

Learning styles best accommodated: Activist, Pragmatist, Reflector

Outcome of learning: Knowledge

Learning resources role: Coordinate development of the program by locating an instructor, scheduling sessions, and publicizing the opportunity.

A real-world economics class is one way to help people grasp the concept of supply and demand and its connection to the price charged for products and the generation of profits.

Johnsonville Sausage contracted with a local college professor to teach a nine-hour program on economics over the course of three months. He illustrated the concept of supply and demand in everyday terms by demonstrating the relationship between the cost of haircuts in the community and the number of haircutting establishments on the town's main street. The instructor then discussed the rudimentary concepts involved in investing in a manufacturing facility—which hypothetically generated low profits, due to the costs of raw materials, labor, overhead, and so on—or making a low-risk investment with a local financial institution. To simulate the decisions a business owner would have to make, participants were given two options: accept the existing low profit level and plan for the next year, or liquidate the company and invest in a money market account that would earn higher short-term profits. More than half the group decided to sell off their assets and take the lower-risk investment with the higher yield. The bottom-line lesson was that without profits, investors have no incentive to keep their money in the company.

Expressing difficult-to-grasp concepts through simplified, real-life examples makes the economics of business easier to understand.

English as a Second Language

Stage for learner: 1, 2, 3, or 4

Context for learning: Formal

Learning styles best accommodated: Activist, Pragmatist

Outcome of learning: Knowledge, Skill Development

Learning resources role: Coordinate program development by locating instructor, scheduling the sessions, and publicizing the opportunity.

TABLE 7 GROUP LEARNING SELECTION

	Stage for Learner	Context for Learning	Complementary Learning Style(s)	Outcome of Learning	Work Related?
Economics 101	1, 2, 3	Formal	Activist, Pragmatist, Reflector	Knowledge	Possibly
English as a Second Language	1, 2, 3, 4	Formal	Activist, Pragmatist	Knowledge, Skill	Yes
Personal Interest Classes–Building Positive Attitudes	1, 2, 3	Formal, Semiformal	Activist, Pragmatist	Knowledge, Skill, Attitude/Values	Possibly
Test-Taking Strategies	2, 3	Formal	Activist, Pragmatist	Knowledge, Skill	No
Learning Networks–Structured Support	3, 4	Nonformal	Activist, Pragmatist, Theorist, Reflector	Knowledge, Skill, Attitude/Values	Yes
Intranet Learning Networks–Online Structured Support	3, 4	Nonformal	Activist, Pragmatist	Knowledge, Skill	Yes
Storytelling–Sharing Organizational Culture	1, 2, 3, 4	Nonformal	Activist, Pragmatist, Theorist, Reflector	Knowledge, Attitude/Values	Yes
Dialogue Groups–Listening to Understand	3, 4	Nonformal	Theorist, Reflector	Knowledge, Attitude/Values	Possibly
Shopping Field Trip for Product Comparison	2, 3	Nonformal	Activist, Pragmatist, Reflector	Knowledge	Yes
Reflective Notes–Analyzing Group Interaction	3, 4	Nonformal	Theorist, Reflector	Knowledge, Skill	Yes
Reading Groups–Promoting Discussion	2, 3, 4	Nonformal	Theorist, Reflector	Knowledge, Skill	Yes
Scan, Clip, and Review–Finding Business Trends	3, 4	Nonformal	Activist, Pragmatist, Theorist, Reflector	Knowledge, Skill	Yes
Business Plan Development–Seeing the Big Picture	2, 3, 4	Nonformal	Activist, Pragmatist, Reflector	Knowledge, Skill	Yes

Technique	Level	Formality	Learning Style	Domain	Recommended
Storyboarding–Envisioning Paths to Future Goals	2, 3, 4	Nonformal	Activist, Pragmatist, Reflector	Knowledge, Attitude/Values	Yes
Guided Imagery–Quick Creative Solutions	2, 3, 4	Nonformal	Pragmatist, Reflector	Aspiration	Possibly
Organizational Lifelines–Reaching a Shared Understanding of Change	2, 3, 4	Nonformal	Activist, Pragmatist, Reflector	Knowledge, Attitude/Values	Yes
Café Society–Conversing with Content Experts	2, 3, 4	Semiformal, Nonformal	Activist, Pragmatist, Theorist, Reflector	Knowledge	Yes
Learning Communities–Real and Virtual Places to Share Interests	2, 3, 4	Nonformal	Activist, Pragmatist, Theorist	Knowledge, Skill	Yes
Fairs and Poster Sessions–Displaying Technologies That Need Champions	2, 3, 4	Nonformal	Activist, Pragmatist, Theorist, Reflector	Knowledge	Yes
Large-Group Processes–Collaborating on Organizational Issues	2, 3, 4	Nonformal	Activist, Pragmatist, Reflector	Knowledge	Yes
External Witnesses–Self-Managed Information Sharing	3, 4	Nonformal	Pragmatist, Theorist, Reflector	Knowledge, Skill	Yes
Live Cases–Strategic Planning and Implementation	3, 4	Nonformal	Activist, Pragmatist, Reflector	Knowledge, Skill	Yes
Groupware–Software Enables Sharing Ideas Across Space and Time	2, 3, 4	Nonformal	Activist, Pragmatist, Theorist, Reflector	Knowledge	Yes
Company Product Workshop–Seeing the Entire Process	1, 2	Formal, Semiformal	Activist, Pragmatist	Knowledge	Yes
Homework Club–Assisting One Another	2, 3	Nonformal	Activist, Pragmatist	Knowledge, Skill	Possibly
Summer Camp for Children	1, 2	Formal, Semiformal	Activist, Pragmatist, Theorist, Reflector	Knowledge, Skill, Attitude/Values, Aspiration	No
School Preparation Day	1, 2, 3, 4	Semiformal	Activist, Pragmatist	Knowledge	No

Many organizations are faced with workers who have limited English skills. This makes it harder for workers to develop on the job and often prevents them from doing the job in the first place. As a result, many organizations have instituted in-house programs for teaching English as a second language.

Some of these programs begin by teaching employees words that apply directly to their work. Taco, Inc., offers five levels of English as a second language. Students are introduced to American history and learn how to deal with their children's schools and manage money (Stewart, 1995). The company also teaches conversational Spanish so that native English speakers can communicate with Spanish-speaking coworkers who are developing English skills.

Personal Interest Classes—Building Positive Attitudes

Stage for learner: 1, 2, or 3

Context for learning: Formal, Semiformal

Learning styles best accommodated: Activist, Pragmatist

Outcome of learning: Knowledge, Skill Development, Attitude/Values

Learning resources role: Coordinate program development by locating an instructor, scheduling sessions, and publicizing the opportunity.

Many companies have developed or hired someone to teach personal interest classes for employees, their spouses, and their children. Some even invite members of the community. Topics include

- *Building basics:* Shop math, assertive communication, effective reading strategies, grammar (sentence structure), grammar (writing process), mathematics refresher, taking minutes or notes

- *Personal:* Quit-smoking programs, personal investment, whale watching (for children), musical instrument lessons, résumé writing, stained glass, drawing, art appreciation, gardening, photography, painting, foreign language, GED preparation, science fair, citizenship, weight watchers, personal fitness

- *Technical:* Fire and safety, measurement, blueprint reading, residential wiring, small-engine repair, technical writing

- *Computer:* How to buy a computer, introduction to computers, introduction to the Internet, keyboarding, introduction to Word, introduction to spreadsheets

Although personal interest classes do not directly benefit the company that sponsors them, they can be of value. "It comes back in the form of attitude. People feel they're playing in the game, not being kicked around in it," says John Hazen White, CEO of Taco, Inc. (Stewart, 1995, p. 75).

Test-Taking Strategies

Stage for learner: 2 or 3

Context for learning: Formal

Learning styles best accommodated: Activist, Pragmatist

Outcome of learning: Knowledge, Skill Development

Learning resources role: Coordinate program development by locating an instructor, scheduling the sessions, and publicizing the opportunity.

At some time, everyone has to take a test. Skill-based pay systems often require tests in order to obtain a pay increase. Individuals may be facing extensive testing for certification by a professional organization or for entrance into a college program. A test-taking strategies session could be helpful for those who have been out of school for a long time or who experience test anxiety.

Learning Networks—Structured Support

Stage for learner: 3 or 4

Context for learning: Nonformal

Learning styles best accommodated: Activist, Pragmatist

Outcome of learning: Knowledge, Skill Development, Attitude/Values

Learning resources role: Coordinate program development, assist in recruiting network members, act as or provide for development of a learning network coach.

As learners begin to manage their own learning, they need support mechanisms to maintain their momentum. Cunningham (1999) created the Learning Sets concept, which has been adopted in a slightly different form by some U.S. companies.

At learning network meetings, employees negotiate new development plans and report on progress. Members of the learning network provide ideas and challenges to their fellow learners. A learning coach, who does not have a learning plan, facilitates discussion. The role of coach can be a learning opportunity in itself for someone who wants to learn facilitation and/or coaching skills.

The learning network is an ongoing process. As one plan is completed, a new one is developed and presented. The network is designed to help members focus on their development by formulating and implementing approaches to specific situations; it also offers support by demonstrating that participants are not alone in facing difficult challenges. Its structure discourages the trading of organizational war stories, which results in little learning and does nothing to change the situation under discussion.

Learning networks must be minimally structured to be effective. Cunningham (1999) recommends a number of guidelines: Networks meet every four to six weeks. At meetings, members work only on practical issues that relate directly to the organization and the needs of the people in the group. The learning network is not a class or a discussion group because it focuses exclusively on learning and development plans.

Essential elements in the meeting structure are

- *Agenda setting:* This should be done at the beginning of the meeting to establish topics to be covered. All members briefly describe what they wish to discuss. A member who has accomplished a lot since the last meeting may ask for more time, whereas another person who is in the middle of a longer project might only want to update the group.

- *Individual time slots:* These are the core learning segments of the meeting. Learners control their own time slots. They decide how to use their time and will adjust the direction of their efforts if the present course has not been effective. During the individual time slot, the four or five other people in the network focus exclusively on what the learner has chosen to bring to the meeting. Each learner should have an individual time slot at each learning network meeting.

- *Process review:* In the early meetings, or at any other time when it seems necessary, a review of the group's working process may be useful. How effective is the network in assisting the learning of its members? Are there ways in which members could be more helpful? Exploring such questions ensures that everyone benefits from the experience.

- *Selection of next meeting date:* At the end of a meeting, members select the next meeting date. Two weeks prior to the date, the learning network coach sends a reminder of the session and solicits agenda items from each member.

Intranet Learning Networks—Online Structured Support

Stage for learner: 3 or 4

Context for learning: Nonformal

Learning styles best accommodated: Activist, Pragmatist,

Outcome of learning: Knowledge, Skill Development

Learning resources role: Coordinate development of program, assist in recruiting network members, act as or provide for development of a learning network coach.

An intranet group functions much like a conventional learning network. A group of people, all of whom are working on their own development, agree to post learning plans and to regularly inform one another of what they have done to achieve their goals. While a facilitator moderates, participants offer coments and suggestions. Instead of meeting together at the same time, network members check in whenever it is convenient.

Storytelling—Sharing Organizational Culture

Stage for learner: 1, 2, 3, or 4

Context for learning: Nonformal

Learning styles best accommodated: Activist, Pragmatist, Theorist, Reflector

Outcome of learning: Knowledge, Attitude/Values

Learning resources role: Coordinate the event by scheduling, publicizing, and locating recorders and facilitators.

Storytelling can be an effective tool for maintaining the history and culture of the company. Participants share those memories of the organization that relate to predetermined themes.

Arrange chairs in a circular format so that people may move to the center to tell their stories. On the outside of the circle, set up one flip chart for each theme to be addressed. These themes could be organizational culture, physical space, leadership, employee base, or some other topic. Find someone to fill the role of the recorder. The record could be pictorial, if the recorder is artistically inclined, or could be composed of short phrases summarizing the story. Set a time limit for the stories— three minutes, for example—and ask the facilitator keep track of the time as well as moderate between stories. When participants finish their stories, they return to the circle and another storyteller comes to the center of the room. There is no feedback or dialogue. It may be helpful to preselect a person with a long institutional memory to begin the storytelling process.

These sessions may be informal and conducted during a lunch hour. They may be held annually as a voluntary activity. Videotape the session so it can be shared with others. I was involved with a storytelling session at The Fielding Institute, a graduate school for mid-career adults, that began with a firsthand account of the founding of the institute. The session continued for about an hour and a half, with faculty, staff, and students telling stories about the changes that have taken place in the organization over the years. The entire event was recorded pictorially in chronological order on a large sheet of butcher paper. It was also videotaped. These two artifacts now serve as historical documents for current and future students, faculty, and staff.

Dialogue Groups—Listening to Understand

Stage for learner: 3 or 4

Context for learning: Nonformal

Learning styles best accommodated: Theorist, Reflector

Outcome of learning: Knowledge, Attitude/Values

Learning resources role: Create and coordinate dialogue group, familiarize participants with the nuances of dialogue.

Dialogue groups provide a forum for discussion and the opportunity to listen with the goal of truly understanding what another person is saying rather than trying to figure out what to say next. One of the main purposes of a dialogue group is to remove blocks to creativity that form when we think we already know the answer. It could be a one-time or ongoing event arranged in dyad or group form.

The word *dialogue* comes from the Greek *dia* (through) and *logos,* (meaning). Participants may have their own opinions about the issue being discussed, but they are willing to be open-minded and suspend judgment in order to learn. In a dialogue, the learner first seeks to understand and then to be understood. The goal is not to be right but to learn from others. For example, when two experts in leadership development met to discuss the benefits of training for leadership development versus a less formal learning approach, each was open to exploring the other's ideas. Neither had formed an opinion on which theory was right and which was wrong, and they were able to explore the concept based on their experiences. As a result, they both learned something new about leadership and learning.

Resources that might be helpful in forming a dialogue group include Pearce and Littlejohn, 1997; Tannen, 1998; and Yankelovich, 1999.

Shopping Field Trip for Product Comparison

Stage for learner: 2 or 3

Context for learning: Nonformal

Learning styles best accommodated: Activist, Pragmatist, Reflector

Outcome of learning: Knowledge

Learning resources role: Suggest activity to leadership, perhaps facilitate the visit.

If you manufacture a product that is distributed for retail sale, take a field trip with a work group to visit a site that sells your or a competitor's product. How is the product merchandized? What is the difference between your product and theirs? What are customers seeing when they shop? How might your product or its presentation be improved?

A service provider might benefit from a similar process. Rather than looking at a physical product, observe the service relationships of a competitor. What can you learn from them?

Reflective Notes—Analyzing Group Interaction

Stage for learner: 3 or 4

Context for learning: Nonformal

Learning styles best accommodated: Theorist, Reflector

Outcome of learning: Knowledge, Skill Development

Learning resources role: Introduce the concept to intact teams, locate or develop a reflective analyst.

Reflective analysis is a tool for capturing and improving group learning (Castleberg, 1999). A reflective analyst attends a meeting to observe its process, interactions, and outcomes. He or she records and interprets key developments. At the end of the meeting, the analyst offers observations, asks questions to help the participants gain new insights into their work, and then writes up his or her comments and distributes them to group members. The next meeting begins with a discussion of the analyst's notes to promote deeper learning. These conversations assist the group in reframing their understanding of the situation and enables them to move forward. The reflective analyst often helps the group discuss the "undiscussables" that hinder performance. Reflective notes are not the same as minutes; they are tools for generating conversations about how individuals in a group work together.

Reading Groups—Promoting Discussion

Stage for learner: 2, 3, or 4

Context for learning: Nonformal

Learning styles best accommodated: Theorist, Reflector

Outcome of learning: Knowledge, Skill Development

Learning resources role: Coordinate development by publicizing, scheduling and facilitating the first session, and obtaining initial reading material; as the group develops, serve as a resource to help locate additional reading material.

Reading a book or article together and then discussing it can be an excellent learning experience. Groups meet biweekly or monthly for as little as one hour.

If group members are not in the habit of reading, you may want to begin with articles from a business magazine. Ask each person to read the assigned material before the meeting. For the first session, the learning resource staff person may function as the facilitator, whose role is to question participants on the reading and how it relates to your business. The idea is to provoke a discussion. Questions may serve to

- Clarify issues

- Guide discussion

- Redirect discussion by asking new questions

- Consolidate and organize issues

- Challenge what is written

- Set up debates

- Push for depth by using phrases such as "tell us more about that" and "what if"

- Ask for analysis

- Ask learners what they would do in a similar situation

- Play devil's advocate and challenge presumptions or present an alternative perspective

- Ask participants to state their assumptions and the grounds for them

In closing, the facilitator reviews the discussion and summarizes the main points. Select another facilitator for the next meeting before disbanding. Rotating the role will increase learning by allowing participants to develop and practice facilitation skills. Initially, learning resources staff may need to meet with facilitators to provide guidance in developing the discussion questions. When participants become comfortable with reading articles, they may be ready to move on to a chapter or section of a business-related book. Limit the group to a maximum of 10 people to ensure that all members will be able to join in the conversation. If more than 10 people are interested, start a second group.

Scan, Clip, and Review—Finding Business Trends

Stage for learner: 3 or 4

Context for learning: Nonformal

Learning styles best accommodated: Activist, Pragmatist, Theorist, Reflector

Outcome of learning: Knowledge, Skill Development

Learning resources role: Coordinate development by publicizing, then scheduling and facilitating the first session.

One way to develop a broader view of your industry or of business trends is to institute a scan, clip, and review team. Each of the five to seven team members subscribes to three business-related magazines. The magazines do not have to be directly connected to your industry. They may even be trade magazines for a totally different industry. The first meeting should occur when the magazines begin to arrive, which should be approximately two months after the subscriptions were sent in.

Members scan their magazines for articles that pique their curiosity. These are clipped out and shared with the group at face-to-face meetings. After all of the articles are shared, the group looks for trends in the information. At each meeting, past trends are compared to new trends. This process may be helpful in identifying promising new lines of business that may warrant future investment. Continue this process over several months.

Business Plan Development—Seeing the Big Picture

Stage for learner: 2, 3, or 4

Context for learning: Nonformal

Learning styles best accommodated: Activist, Pragmatist, Reflector

Outcome of learning: Knowledge, Skill Development

Learning resources role: Coordinate development by publicizing, scheduling sessions, identifying product to be developed, and facilitating first meeting. As group progresses, provide assistance with locating additional resources.

Business plan development is a process that not only may help people to learn but may have an additional positive impact on the organization. Create a voluntary team to write a business plan for a product or service. Gather a group from various areas of the organization or try the process with an existing work group. The idea is that before the group can write a business plan, the members will have to learn about every facet of the company because they must address all aspects in the overall plan.

The group could meet every other week in the evening after a light dinner. Formal presentations should focus on the components of a business plan, and participants should research all elements of the business plan themselves. If members are planning a new product, they would identify different ways of presenting the product, solicit customer viewpoints, and investigate details such as the cost of machinery needed to make the product or its packaging.

Rotate the leadership role according to each participants' expertise. For example, a production worker could lead the discussion on the manufacturing process, a warehouser might address storage concerns, an accountant could provide guidance on costs, and a salesperson might speak knowledgeably about sales techniques. As a result, participants will assemble a clearer picture of the entire organization's functioning and will understand how their jobs fit into the bigger picture.

Storyboarding—Envisioning Paths to Future Goals

> **Stage for learner:** 2, 3, or 4
>
> **Context for learning:** Nonformal
>
> **Learning styles best accommodated:** Activist, Pragmatist, Reflector
>
> **Outcome of learning:** Knowledge, Attitude/Values
>
> **Learning resources role:** Set up process, procure paper and markers, facilitate the session.

Storyboarding is the process of graphically illustrating a vision either for the future of the organization or for a product line. Glaxo Wellcome has found that storyboards encourage creativity (Godfrey, 1998).

Begin in a large room without tables or chairs. Set the mood with light background music. Provide each participant with a felt-tip marker and a large sheet of paper divided into six blank boxes.

Ask each person to envision the future of the organization, department, or product line. A facilitator may need to stimulate the creative process with a brainstorming session. When the participants are ready, ask them to draw a picture of their interpretation of the future in Box 6. When this is done, instruct them to return to Box 1 and draw a picture of how things are today. Next, they would use Boxes 2 through 5 to depict the transition from Box 1 to Box 6. After participants have completed their storyboards, they share their hopes for the fulfillment of the future they have drawn.

This process can be undertaken either individually or as a group to develop the team's view of the future. Individuals may discover how to fulfill goals, and team members may achieve a clearer perception of the commonalities and differences among them.

Guided Imagery—Quick Creative Solutions

Stage for learner: 2, 3, or 4

Context for learning: Nonformal

Learning styles best accommodated: Theorist, Reflector

Outcome of learning: Aspiration

Learning resources role: Lead the imaging session; procure paper and markers.

With tranquil music in the background, use a soothing voice to take people on an imaginary trip through a garden. At the end of the walk, ask them to look at a problem and imagine the possible solutions. Provide markers and paper so participants can capture their thoughts. This process may sound a bit corny, but it has been used with great success at Glaxo Wellcome. One participant stated, "I achieved in 20 minutes what I estimated would take me two days to do" (Godfrey, 1998, p. 15).

Organizational Lifelines— Reaching a Shared Understanding of Change

Stage for learner: 2, 3, or 4

Context for learning: Nonformal

Learning styles best accommodated: Activist, Pragmatist, Reflector

Outcome of learning: Knowledge, Attitude/Values

Learning resources role: Set up process, procure paper and markers, facilitate the session.

An organizational lifeline depicts an individual perspective on changes in the organization. Each lifeline begins with the participant's first day on the job and goes on to note major events within the organization or a specific department. This process combines many individual lifelines to create a composite view of the organization.

Participants are given markers and paper and asked to draw pictures of significant learning events in their working lives. The facilitator should explain that the exercise is not concerned with artistic ability but is designed to identify those points at which learning has occurred. Participants are allowed half an hour to develop their organizational lifelines, then 10 minutes to share their lifelines with the rest of the group. The facilitator asks questions about the similarities and differences in the participant's perspectives and helps the group combine their individual views into a shared understanding of the organization.

Café Society—Conversing with Content Experts

Stage for learner: 2, 3, or 4

Context for learning: Semiformal, Nonformal

Learning styles best accommodated: Activist, Pragmatist, Theorist, Reflector

Outcome of learning: Knowledge

Learning resources role: Set up process, introduce session and content experts.

A Parisian café provides the model for the café society, which can be applied in a conference setting (Cunningham, Bennett, and Dawes, 2000). The café society is an informal, unstructured environment in which people may converse about a common topic with a content expert from inside or outside the organization.

Post the event's theme on a flip chart or project it from a transparency. The topic could be general, such as knowledge management, or more specific, such as techniques for providing performance feedback.

Furnish the meeting room with round tables surrounded by six to eight chairs. Seat one content expert at each table and display the expert's name and area of expertise on a placard. A learning resources staff person could introduce the experts and announce their areas of expertise, which would be the focus of conversation at the various tables. Invite participants to sit at any table and then move to another one when they feel they have enough information. Only the content experts remain at the same table for the entire event. Allow two hours for the session so that everyone has a chance to visit areas of interest. This process allows participants to engage in a dialogue with experts instead of simply listening to a formal presentation.

Learning Communities—
Real and Virtual Places to Share Interests

Stage for learner: 2, 3, or 4

Context for learning: Nonformal

Learning styles best accommodated: Activist, Pragmatist, Theorist

Outcome of learning: Knowledge, Skill Development

Learning resources role: Facilitate the process.

A learning community is a real or virtual place where people gather to share ideas and contacts and set up special interest groups. The Fielding Institute's Organization Design and Effectiveness master's degree program has a Web site called Community Hall, which allows learning groups to post topics of interest so that interaction and dialogue may take place. A similar process could occur in a conference setting, using open-space technology—people would identify interesting subjects and meet to discuss them and, if feasible, develop ideas for action (Owen, 1997).

Fairs and Poster Sessions—
Displaying Technologies That Need Champions

Stage for learner: 2, 3, or 4

Context for learning: Nonformal

Learning styles best accommodated: Activist, Pragmatist, Theorist, Reflector

Outcome of learning: Knowledge

Learning resources role: Coordinate the poster presentations and set up fairs.

In an effort to provide opportunities for innovation, 3M hosts fairs to introduce technologies in need of champions to sponsor or advocate product development (Brand, 1998). People with potential projects are available to visitors of diverse backgrounds, who are invited to join them and examine these opportunities. The face-to-face environment often generates more ideas.

In an alternative event, the poster fair, participants create posters depicting their current work. Visitors view the posters and ask questions to learn more about the participants and their projects.

Large-Group Processes—
Collaborating on Organizational Issues

Stage for learner: 2, 3, or 4

Context for learning: Nonformal

Learning styles best accommodated: Activist, Pragmatist, Reflector

Outcome of learning: Knowledge

Learning resources role: Coordinate and facilitate process.

Sainsbury, an accounting firm in the United Kingdom, held a one-day planning event to encourage a collaborative approach to organizational issues (Cunningham, Bennett, and Dawes, 2000). Approximately 80 people began the day with an overview of the event. Organizers used a collage depicting the past, present, and future of the group to draw attention to current issues. Participants broke into small groups to define and prioritize areas of concern, which they listed on flip charts and posted on the wall where everyone could read them. From those lists, the entire group selected the most crucial issues,. Dividing back into small groups, the participants then redefined and consolidated. Participants were free to move from one group to another. The large group met again to refine the list of topics and share new concerns that had emerged during the discussions. After the large group meeting, participants separated into small, self-selected groups for a third time to further define the issues. Next, the whole body met to determine which issues could be solved on the spot and which required additional attention. Action teams were formed to develop approaches and solutions. A final, large-group session worked on assigning responsibilities and establishing a schedule for feedback.

In large-group meetings such as this, flexibility is key. While the facilitators of such an event might enter the project with a plan in mind, they must remain flexibile enough to respond to issues as they arise. Large groups include many people in the process, which is a major advantage. This creates a greater sense of ownership among the participants and generates a good deal of positive energy. For additional information on large-group interventions, see Weisbord and Janoff (1995) on search conferences, Emery and Emery (1976) on future search, and Owen (1997) on the use of open space.

External Witnesses–
Self-Managed Information Sharing

Stage for learner: 3 or 4

Context for learning: Nonformal

Learning styles best accommodated: Pragmatist, Theorist, Reflector

Outcome of learning: Knowledge, Skill Development

Learning resources role: Locate external witnesses, coordinate and facilitate the session.

External witnesses are an alternative to presentations by content experts on their areas of expertise. This process involves a more self-managed form of information sharing (Cramb and Cunningham, 1998).

KPMG's audit, tax, and consulting partners were interested in learning from three external experts employed at service businesses that were unlike KPMG. The external witnesses functioned as a panel. Participants asked them questions, exploring the similarities and differences in their approaches. Surprisingly, the witnesses used divergent approaches to describe the same thing. For instance, one answered questions by telling stories and another used rich metaphors although his organization's communication style was literal and analytical.

After the question-and-answer session, small groups examined the differences in style, context, and content. A major advantage to this approach is that it avoids possibly boring presentations because presenters focus on matters of concern to participants. It also encourages participants to be responsible for eliciting from witnesses the content that is most useful for them.

Live Cases—Strategic Planning and Implementation

Stage for learner: 3 or 4

Context for learning: Nonformal

Learning styles best accommodated: Activist, Pragmatist, Reflector

Outcome of learning: Knowledge, Skill Development

Learning resources role: Locate case presenters, coordinate and facilitate the session.

Standardized case studies, such as those used in business schools, are based on past situations. They do not allow learners to delve into the real development of the case or interact with those who were involved. Live cases may be used to help people understand strategy and its implementation (Cunningham, Bennett, and Dawes, 2000).

At one company that used this technique, the chief executive officer of another company was asked to produce financial statements and other pertinent corporate facts, such as market information, to describe his company's condition five years earlier. A resource person gave participants a quick overview of strategy theory. The CEO then provided a five-minute introduction to his company. Small groups went over material they had received in advance and developed questions for the CEO about the state of the business five years ago.

The questioning took place in a large-group format. Afterwards, participants separated into small groups to work on developing a strategy they thought the CEO should have adopted. Returning to a large-group format, participants presented their plans to the CEO. The CEO responded by sharing with them what actually had been done and providing current financial and other data about the company. The session concluded with a general discussion of what had been learned.

This approach helps individuals and groups deepen their understanding of strategic planning and implementation.

Groupware—Software Enables
Sharing Ideas Across Space and Time

Stage for learner: 2, 3, or 4

Context for learning: Nonformal

Learning styles best accommodated: Activist, Pragmatist, Theorist,
Reflector

Outcome of learning: Knowledge

Learning resources role: Identify possibility, coordinate with organizational leadership in development, provide training.

Groupware is software that helps groups of people work together and
learn from one another. A team room, for instance, allows people to
share ideas and information despite the barriers of time and distance. At
Johnsonville Sausage, teams post their major projects on the company
intranet each week. Everyone in the organization then has access to current information on a regular basis. Internal customers learn about their
internal suppliers' projects via groupware.

Company Product Workshop—
Seeing the Entire Process

Stage for learner: 1 or 2

Context for learning: Formal, Semiformal

Learning styles best accommodated: Activist, Pragmatist

Outcome of learning: Knowledge

Learning resources role: Locate presenters and facilitate development
of the workshop.

People who make a product or provide a service often see only one piece
of a much larger picture. A workshop about company products expands
their perceptions to include the entire product or process.

YSI, Inc., manufactures scientific instruments. Many workers are
involved in assembling an instrument, yet they do not know how the fin-

ished product is used. The product knowledge workshop gives them the whole picture. Then when a quality issue comes up, they are better able to understand what is required and make changes (Honold, 1999).

Homework Club–Assisting One Another

> **Stage for learner:** 2 or 3
>
> **Context for learning:** Nonformal
>
> **Learning styles best accommodated:** Activist, Pragmatist
>
> **Outcome of learning:** Knowledge, Skill Development
>
> **Learning resources role:** Arrange for or be a resource for the group.

Learners in the same class or program at a local school may benefit from a semi-structured environment in which to study and do homework together. The learners could help one another, with a resource person or facilitator available to assist when needed.

Involving Children

Getting employees' children to learn can make parents more willing to learn. A summer camp for children and a school preparation day are possible ways to begin this process.

Summer Camp for Children

> **Stage for learner:** 1 or 2
>
> **Context for learning:** Formal, Semiformal
>
> **Learning styles best accommodated:** Activist, Pragmatist, Theorist, Reflector
>
> **Outcome of learning:** Knowledge, Skill Development, Attitude/Values, Aspiration
>
> **Learning resources role:** Coordinate development of program by locating an instructor, scheduling sessions, and publicizing the opportunity.

As an alternative to day care, Taco, Inc., provides a summer camp for employees' children. The day camp is scheduled for the same hours as the parent's work schedule. It offers programs on subjects such as oceanography, art, music, and drama. Taco, Inc., contracts with local educational institutions to present the program. If the camps are located off-site, the company provides transportation.

School Preparation Day

Stage for learner: 1, 2, 3, or 4

Context for learning: Semiformal

Learning styles best accommodated: Activist, Pragmatist

Outcome of learning: Knowledge

Learning resources role: Coordinate teachers' visits, set up refresher courses.

Select an August date for teachers from various grades in your local school district to come in and talk to employees and their children about the curricula for the coming year.

Alternatively, the learning resources staff could obtain information on the curricula for K–12 from the local school district. The staff could set up refresher courses for parents who are interested in helping their children with homework. This would benefit children, parents, the school district, and the company.

10

Tools and Strategies for Integrating Learning with Work

An organization's ability to learn, and translate that learning into action rapidly, is the ultimate competitive business advantage.

JACK WELCH
Business Week

A poultry company wanted to increase production quality. Under its pay-for-skill system, workers received raises as their contribution to the company increased. At the third level of this system, each employee took a quality class and completed a project that explored improvement to quality or production processes. Employees consulted with their supervisors to confirm that their projects would not conflict with any quality-program components, such as USDA requirements. Then they thoroughly researched the issues, developed solutions, and presented their project to a management team. Projects that presented feasible proposals were approved, and employees worked with their supervisors to implement their ideas. The purpose of this project was to ensure the employees' understanding of the work process, the quality program, and customer requirements for the product.

Introduction to Integrating Learning into Work

One of the issues faced by many human resources development professionals is how to go about integrating learning into work. Individual learning in the workplace often happens when we confront a problem.

How we respond to problems makes the difference between learning and not learning. In the above situation, longer-term employees might have accompanied new operators as they worked through their problems; however, when people are responsible for their own learning, the chances are greater that what they learn will stay with them. Employees who learn in context, by choosing to integrate learning into their everyday experiences on the job, may not need a teacher at all.

The underlying premise of this approach, known as action learning, is that action and learning are reciprocal. Learning requires action, and action requires learning (Lankard, 1995). Action learning generally takes place among a small group of people who are concerned about the issue, have information to contribute, and are in a position to implement a recommended solution (Marquardt, 1999). Its aim is to develop solutions to existing problems, which means it often occurs when it is needed, not beforehand. Yet, despite its focus, problem solving is not the outcome—learning is.

Reflection is the critical element. Afterwards, those who played a part in resolving the situation reflect on how they did it—systemically recalling what was done, analyzing each step through questioning and discussion, and forming a shared understanding of the process. They concentrate not on what they did but on how they did it.

In addition to problem solving, action learning can be used for team building, leadership development, and professional growth and development.

According to Lankard (1995), the conditions necessary for action learning are

- *Proactivity:* We must take charge of our own learning and determine how we can learn from a situation. If we do not, we might learn little or nothing from the experience.

- *Critical reflection:* We must look back at an experience critically and ask ourselves, "What have I learned from this?" Combining reflective and action learning concepts with individual learning keeps us moving forward on a learning curve. Many believe that reflecting on what we have learned results in the most effective learning (Argyris and Schön, 1974; Brookfield, 1991; Schön, 1983).

- *Creativity:* In order to learn something, we must see situations in a different light. We must be creative in our thinking about where learning can occur.

Characteristics of Group Learning

As you go about the selection process for your learning system, you may decide to offer many types of learning to accomodate multiple learning styles and to vary the degree of relationship to the workplace. Table 8 on pages 174 and 175 lists all the group learning tools in this chapter and is designed to assist you with your selections.

Learning Tools

Organizations create opportunities for intentional learning in context in a number of ways.

Mistakes as Learning Indicators

Stage for learner: 1, 2, 3, or 4

Context for learning: Nonformal

Learning styles best accommodated: Activist, Pragmatist, Theorist, Reflector

Outcome of learning: Knowledge

Learning resources role: Continually reinforce value of learning from mistakes, circulate articles such as "No More Mistakes and You're Through!"

John Cleese (1988) wrote an article that appeared in *Forbes* magazine entitled "No More Mistakes and You're Through!" His argument was that if you are not making mistakes, you are not taking risks. If you are not taking risks, you probably are not learning or improving yourself. Businesses cannot afford to stand still. Therefore, Cleese concluded, anyone who is not learning and improving should not be part of the organization. A former employer told me, on my first day on the job, "As of today, you are becoming obsolete—unless you do something to improve yourself." He expected learning and growth and knew mistakes might be a part of the process.

Some companies develop specific statements about their tolerance of mistakes. One of the classic examples of the value of learning from mistakes occurred at 3M. The Post-it® Note was reportedly created when an employee identified another use for an adhesive that was too weak for the original application (Brand, 1998).

TABLE 8   INTEGRATING LEARNING WITH WORK

LEARNING IN CONTEXT

	Stage for Learner	Context for Learning	Complementary Learning Style(s)	Outcome of Learning	Work Related?
Mistakes as Learning Indicators	1, 2, 3, 4	Nonformal	Activist, Pragmatist, Theorist, Reflector	Knowledge	Yes
Problem Solving–Not Only for Leaders	1, 2, 3, 4	Nonformal, Informal	Activist, Pragmatist, Theorist, Reflector	Knowledge, Skill	Yes
CAMP–for Foreign Cultural Experience	3, 4	Formal, Semiformal	Activist, Pragmatist, Reflector	Knowledge, Skill, Attitude/Values	Yes
Team Development Plans– Improving Collaboration with an Outside Facilitator	3, 4	Nonformal	Activist, Pragmatist, Reflector	Knowledge, Skill	Yes
Think Tanks–Action Forums to Improve Company Performance	3, 4	Semiformal, Nonformal	Activist, Pragmatist, Reflector	Knowledge, Skill	Yes
Customer Champions–Facilitating Resolution of Customer Issues	2, 3	Nonformal	Activist, Pragmatist, Reflector	Knowledge, Skill	Yes
Team Projects–Developing New Products	2, 3, 4	Nonformal	Activist, Pragmatist, Theorist, Reflector	Knowledge, Skill	Yes
Attending Meetings–Reflecting on Group Interaction	3, 4	Nonformal	Theorist, Reflector	Knowledge, Skill	Yes
Reflective Note Taking–Seeing Interaction Patterns	3, 4	Nonformal	Theorist, Reflector	Knowledge, Skill	Yes
Financial Meetings–Relating Performance to Goals	1, 2, 3	Semiformal	Activist, Pragmatist, Reflector	Knowledge, Skill	Yes

Activity		Formality	Learning Styles	Type	
Employee-Led Meetings–Company Performance in Employees' Words	1, 2, 3, 4	Nonformal	Activist, Pragmatist, Reflector	Knowledge, Skill	Yes
Meeting Assessment–Attendees' Analysis	2, 3, 4	Semiformal	Theorist, Reflector	Knowledge	Yes
Meeting Check-in–Briefly Identifying Mental States	1, 2, 3, 4	Semiformal	Activist, Reflector	Knowledge, Attitude/Values	Yes
Meeting Checkout–Quick Results Focus	1, 2, 3, 4	Semiformal	Activist, Reflector	Knowledge, Attitude/Values	Yes
Building Consensus–No One Actively Opposes Decision	1, 2, 3, 4	Semiformal	Activist, Pragmatist, Theorist	Knowledge, Skill	Yes
Establishing and Maintaining Ground Rules	1, 2, 3, 4	Semiformal	Activist, Pragmatist, Reflector	Knowledge, Skill	Yes
Brainstorming–Generating Creative Ideas	1, 2, 3, 4	Semiformal	Activist, Pragmatist	Knowledge	Yes
Knowledge Networks–Sharing Tacit Knowledge in a Database	3, 4	Nonformal	Theorist, Reflector	Knowledge	Yes
Whiteboards–Capturing Ideas Generated in the Cafeteria	3, 4	Nonformal	Theorist, Reflector	Knowledge	Yes

The management of the Harley-Davidson Motor Company has incorporated mistakes into their shared vision. They believe that if the company is to be effective, it must seek out the causes of mistakes and failures as well as of successes (Solomon, 1994). The use of mistakes as opportunities for learning starts at the top of the organization. A now-retired CEO began an executive meeting by stating, "Here's something I screwed up on this week—and here's what I learned from it" (Van de Kamp Nohl, 2000, p. 17).

With the assistance of a trainer or safety coordinator, employees at Wainwright Industries videotape reenactments of all accidents and near-accidents (Honold, 1999). They play the tape, which is narrated by those involved in the incident, at departmental meetings for everyone who might have to face a similar situation.

At Buckman Laboratories, mistakes are valued as a source of new ideas. They can be used to generate innovative solutions to problems (Pan and Scarborough, 1998).

Problem Solving—Not Only for Leaders

Stage for learner: 1, 2, 3, or 4

Context for learning: Nonformal, Informal

Learning styles best accommodated: Activist, Pragmatist, Reflector

Outcome of learning: Knowledge, Skill Development

Learning resources role: Reinforce value of learning through problem solving.

Ralph Stayer, CEO of Johnsonville Sausage, quips, "Managers and leaders are a bundle of solutions trying to find problems to attach themselves to." More can be learned if leaders allow others to resolve issues. To transform problem resolution into a learning tool, leaders must define the parameters within which employees are allowed to make decisions. Are there budget constraints for solutions to potential problems? If so, what are they?

In planning changes to their compensation system, one organization told a project team that any compensation system would be acceptable as long as it treated employees fairly, paid the average rate for the local labor market, and based wage increases on increased value of labor to the company. With these minimal constraints, the team designed a system that fit the needs of the organization and its employees.

The manager of any department in which changes may occur should be available as a resource if employees need assistance.

CAMP—for Foreign Cultural Experience

Stage for learner: 3 or 4

Context for learning: Formal, Semiformal

Learning styles best accommodated: Activist, Pragmatist, Reflector

Outcome of learning: Knowledge, Skill Development, Attitude/Values

Learning resources role: Create or facilitate creation of program, assist in selecting participants, coordinate the various phases.

Motorola University created a cultural experiences program for employees who were being assignd to other countries (McCain and Pantazis, 1997). The China Accelerated Management Program (CAMP) runs through five phases over a 12-month period. Phase 1 consists of classroom teaching about the country, its culture, its ethics, and its management tools. It concludes with a site visit to the country. Phase 2 consists of an on-the-job action learning program. Phase 3 provides training in leadership, influence skills, and project management. Participants then spend six weeks in job rotation to another country. During Phase 4, participants select a specific skill they learned in CAMP and teach it to other employees or suppliers. Phase 5 provides a business simulation assessment to identify future skill development needs. A graduation ceremony celebrates the completion of the program.

Team Development Plans—Improving Collaboration with an Outside Facilitator

Stage for learner: 3 or 4

Context for learning: Nonformal

Learning styles best accommodated: Activist, Pragmatist, Reflector

Outcome of learning: Knowledge, Skill Development

Learning resources role: Develop or obtain assessment form, publicize availability of the program, act as outside facilitator for the process.

Teams, like individuals, may benefit from the creation and use of development plans. A marketing team for a manufacturer used an assessment form like the one in Exercise 5 to determine how well they were working together. Afterwards, they developed a plan for improving the quality of their collaboration.

Team members filled out the forms and gave them to an outside facilitator, who provided feedback at a team meeting. The facilitator then led a discussion to determine the team's perception of the answers they had given in the assessment forms. The team decided there was one main issue—they were unable to challenge one another, which led to an inability to engage in truly developmental discussions. The group brainstormed methods of developing themselves in this area, agreed on an approach, and moved forward.

The type of instrument shown in Exercise 5 may be used for development of a functional work group or a cross-functional team. Although the group is responsible for developing its own solution to the developmental need, it may draw on outside expertise to do so. The process may be repeated every six months, which should allow enough time to address one area before moving on to another one.

Think Tanks—Action Forums to Improve Company Performance

Stage for learner: 3 or 4

Context for learning: Semiformal, Nonformal

Learning styles best accommodated: Activist, Pragmatist, Reflector

Outcome of learning: Knowledge, Skill Development

Learning resources role: Coordinate creation, facilitate action forum process.

Pacific Gas & Electric Company's action forum process was created to solve problems but also led to cost savings and learning for those involved (Flynn, 1996). The process has three distinct phases: framework, action forum, and accountability.

The framework phase involves preparation. A management team focuses on and clearly defines the issue, interviews all stakeholders (employees and customers), invites key players to become team members of the action forum, and selects a champion who can rally the team to

EXERCISE 5: TEAM ASSESSMENT FORM

Team: _____ Date _____

Circle the number that indicates the extent to which you agree or disagree with
following statements.

	Strongly Agree	Agree	Disagree	Strongly Disagree
1. Common goal: Our team is completely unified. We know where we are going and how we will get there.	1	2	3	4
2. Full participation: All members contribute to our team when they have something to contribute. We share ideas freely and openly.	1	2	3	4
3. Confronting differences: All members feel free to confront and challenge one another. We avoid blaming one another.	1	2	3	4
4. Mutual support: We have a common bond and sense of belonging. People offer help without being asked. We each verbally recognize the performance of others.	1	2	3	4
5. Commitment to our decisions: People are genuinely committed to the decisions we make together.	1	2	3	4
6. Checking our effectiveness: We perform frequent process checks. We have a process in place that enables us to track our progress.	1	2	3	4
7. Team development: Team development is a regular part of our meeting process.	1	2	3	4
8. Leadership: We work together as a team. Everyone has an opportunity for leadership.	1	2	3	4
9. Open communication: Communication is open and honest. We welcome feedback, both as a group and as individuals.	1	2	3	4
10. Balance: We balance between focusing on our task and focusing on the needs of people.	1	2	3	4
11. Flexibility and creativity: We are flexible, creative, and experimental in the way we do things.	1	2	3	4
12. Listening: We actively listen to one another. When we do not understand something, we say so. We ask nonjudgmental questions.	1	2	3	4
13. Openness to change: We accept and look forward to change with enthusiasm.	1	2	3	4
14. Checking customer satisfaction: We frequently solicit feedback on our performance from our internal and external customers.	1	2	3	4

action. The management team also selects a separate cross-functional leadership team that will either approve any plan developed by the action forum or send it back to the team for additional work. During the framework phase, team members gather all the data they believe they will need for the second stage, the action forum.

The action forum takes place off-site at a company learning center. These two- to three-day think-tank sessions begin with brainstorming. The team, which may consist of up to 70 people, identifies problems, prioritizes them, and develops creative action plans for improvements. During this process, every idea is transformed into a visual image using adhesive notes, index cards, and flip charts. Trained facilitators, who are not team members, keep the process moving. The team refines and develops each plan to fit an implementation period of no more than 90 days. During the last few hours of the forum, the team presents the action plans and timelines to the cross-functional leadership team. The leadership team must make an immediate decision on each plan. If they deny a plan, they must give their reasons. If they say maybe, they must explain what needs to be done and establish a deadline.

In the third, or accountability, phase, the role of the team champion becomes critical as the team implements its plan. The champion keeps the team to the agreed-upon time frame. At 30 days, and again at 60 days, the action forum team meets with the leadership team to share what has been done and hear any recommendations for changes in tactics. They meet again at 90 days for a report and a celebration.

In more than 80 action forums, the company has saved at least $270 million through cycle-time reduction, productivity improvements, cost avoidance, cost reductions, and earnings improvement (Flynn, 1996). The company believes some elements are critical to the success of the think-tank process.

- The sessions are voluntary and organic, not required.

- There is no formal training for how to be involved. People learn the process as they go along.

- Think tanks are never used to eliminate jobs; they focus on improving the business.

- Cost savings from action forums do not affect the group's operating budget.

Customer Champions–
Facilitating Resolution of Customer Issues

Stage for learner: 2 or 3

Context for learning: Nonformal

Learning styles best accommodated: Activist, Pragmatist, Reflector

Outcome of learning: Knowledge, Skill Development

Learning resources role: Coordinate program development in conjunction with quality staff.

Wainwright Industries uses the concept of champions to provide superior service to their customers (Honold, 1999). Each year, employees, and sometimes production associates, are selected by the customer service manager and the production manager to be champions for each of the company's major customers. It is a voluntary role. If they accept, they attend a short training class presented by the customer service and quality managers to learn the reponsibilities of customer champions and approaches to finding the root cause of a problem.

Whenever a customer voices a concern, the champion is responsible for gathering the appropriate group of people—from management and production—to address the issue. Customers are asked to fill out quarterly report cards on the company's performance. Any low marks are turned over to customer champions, who do not have to solve the problems but attempt to facilitate a resolution. By the end of a year, champions know a great deal more about the product, the customers' needs, and the company itself.

Team Projects–Developing New Products

Stage for learner: 2, 3, or 4

Context for learning: Nonformal

Learning styles best accommodated: Activist, Pragmatist, Theorist, Reflector

Outcome of learning: Knowledge, Skill Development

Learning resources role: Possibly assist group facilitator in learning facilitation skills.

Working together in a group is an effective way to gain new skills. YSI, Inc., develops new products through team projects (Honold, 1999). Members of the team come from all areas of the company that may be directly involved with the new product: marketing, engineering, production, customer service, purchasing, quality, and so on. The group's facilitator is generally a manager. Members are responsible for ensuring that the functions of their units are covered in the plan. The group designs the product and researches all aspects of the market before presenting it to the top management team for approval.

Two kinds of learning occur in YSI's new product teams: functional and relational. Functional learning leads to an understanding of how each unit affects the product and fits into the entire organization. Relational learning develops the skills needed to work together as a group. The team process could also be used in address improvements in products or services.

Attending Meetings—Reflecting on Group Interaction

Stage for learner: 3 or 4

Context for learning: Nonformal

Learning styles best accommodated: Theorist, Reflector

Outcome of learning: Knowledge, Skill Development

Learning resources role: Coach learner in techniques for learning from meetings, provide reflection form.

Meetings can provide rich opportunities for learning if the learner is aware of the process. While attending a meeting, a learner should pay attention to group dynamics. As soon as possible after the meeting, the learner reflects on what he or she has observed by asking the following questions:

- Which company norms were evident in this meeting?

- What could I tell about company/departmental priorities as a result of this meeting?

- When a problem or conflict arose, what skills/processes were used to address it?

- Did people collaborate? Was there conflict? Around which issues did collaboration and/or conflict arise?

- Did people listen to one another? How was this shown?

- How did the work of this meeting affect the bigger picture of this organization?

A learning resources specialist could design a reflection form with the above questions to assist in the process.

Reflective Note Taking—Seeing Interaction Patterns

Stage for learner: 3 or 4

Context for learning: Nonformal

Learning styles best accommodated: Reflector, Theorist

Outcome of learning: Knowledge, Skill Development

Learning resources role: Coach learner on techniques for learning from meetings, provide reflection form.

Originally, outside observers used reflective notetaking to help groups learn more effectively (Castleberg, 1999; see also Reflective Notes in Chapter 9). It may also be used as a tool for learning while attending department meetings.

During the meeting, watch what happens and take notes on such questions as these: Who is speaking? Who is not? What is being said? What comes up but is not addressed? Over time, do you see a pattern in what is addressed and what is not? How might you affect the group's effectiveness? After the meeting, reflect on your notes. What are the patterns? After several meetings, distinct patterns will emerge.

Financial Meetings—Relating Performance to Goals

Stage for learner: 1, 2, or 3

Context for learning: Semiformal

Learning styles best accommodated: Activist, Pragmatist, Reflector

Outcome of learning: Knowledge, Skill Development

Learning resources role: Assist in creating system.

"Employees are better able to perform when they understand business strategy and the real problems faced in implementing it," says Jack Stack (1998). He believes that the best way for employees to learn about business basics is to understand the company's financial performance in relation to its goals. A formal meeting system is a key element in this process (Honold, 1999).

At the first meeting of plant leadership, department supervisors relate department performance to goals by posting modified profit-and-loss statements where everyone can see them. The statements illustrate month-to-date and year-to-date performance and explain any performance that is 5% more or less than the goal.

At the next meeting, plant managers report plant performance data and explain any significant variances to company leadership. A participant records the data with a laptop computer and projects it onto a screen. The information is printed out and disseminated to all managers. Before the end of the week, the managers meet with their departments to share the financial data with all employees. They explain each line on the profit-and-loss statement so that everyone is aware of the company's performance, where the problem spots are, and how the work of each individual contributes to the information presented.

Employee-Led Meetings— Company Performance in Employees' Words

Stage for learner: 1, 2, 3, or 4

Context for learning: Nonformal

Learning styles best accommodated: Activist, Pragmatist, Reflector

Outcome of learning: Knowledge, Skill Development

Learning resources role: Assist in coordinating event, provide assistance to speakers in developing presentations.

The annual Johnsonville Sausage Great Performance Meetings are company-wide gatherings. Employees, rather than top management, lead these meetings, which inform members about the company's performance.

In 1998, for example, a sausage stuffer and a worker at the company's raw materials plant stood in front of 425 other participants and presented a report on the accomplishments their cross-functional team. The raw materials team got a standing ovation for their success the previous year. To quote a production member, "Our GP meeting is what we have done . . . what [we] did, what [we] learned to become better in our results. . . . The last GP meeting was the best one we have ever had. It was people from out in the plant, working on the line, telling stories of how they became great or how they can become great. These people aren't professional speakers. They didn't go to school for this stuff. They got up and talked like a plant person and others can relate to that" (Pennings, 1998). After the reports, employees and leadership asked questions about the company and its operations. Problems, if any, were taken back to the relevant facility to be resolved. Participants reacted positively to members describing their own successes and to the learning gained from putting together the presentations. Other organizations may benefit from a similarly dynamic and interactive approach to company meetings.

Meeting Assessment—Attendees' Analysis

Stage for learner: 2, 3, or 4

Context for learning: Semiformal

Learning styles best accommodated: Theorist, Reflector

Outcome of learning: Knowledge

Learning resources role: Provide list of questions for attendees' use in meeting assessment.

At the end of each meeting, spend five minutes assessing the meeting process and discussing how to improve it in the future. Questions could be, How did this meeting go? What did we do well? What could we improve on? How could we better manage ourselves so that the next meeting goes more smoothly and accomplishes more?

Meeting Check-in—Briefly Identifying Mental States

Stage for learner: 1, 2, 3, or 4

Context for learning: Semiformal

Learning styles best accommodated: Activist, Reflector

Outcome of learning: Knowledge, Attitude/Values

Learning resources role: Provide brief instructions for check-in.

A check-in is a way of refocusing on the meeting and learning about the mental states of other attendees. All participants take one minute or less to identify whatever thoughts were distracting or preoccupying them when they entered the meeting. This time should be spent on uninterrupted private reflection. Check-in statements may reveal anything from family or work concerns to commuter frustration; however, this is not a time to engage in conversation about personal matters. The purpose of the check-in is to become aware of and understand the unseen factors that may interfere with another person's participation.

Meeting Checkout—Quick Results Focus

> **Stage for learner:** 1, 2, 3, or 4
>
> **Context for learning:** Semiformal
>
> **Learning styles best accommodated:** Activist, Reflector
>
> **Outcome of learning:** Knowledge, Attitude/Values
>
> **Learning resources role:** Provide brief instructions for checkout.

At the conclusion of a meeting, a checkout enables participants to focus quickly on what they learned, both personally and in terms of the corporation. In one minute or less, each attendee briefly describes what was most valuable or frustrating about the meeting. Begin the checkout by asking, What did you get out of this meeting? What will you do as a result of it?

Building Consensus—No One Actively Opposes Decision

> **Stage for learner:** 1, 2, 3, or 4
>
> **Context for learning:** Semiformal
>
> **Learning styles best accommodated:** Activist, Pragmatist, Theorist
>
> **Outcome of learning:** Knowledge, Skill Development
>
> **Learning resources role:** Provide brief directions, facilitate process while participants learn it.

Building consensus means reaching a decision that can be supported by all the participants. While there may be some who think there is a better alternative, no member of the group actively opposes a decision made by consensus. Consensus does not mean everyone is in full agreement or is totally satisfied, nor does it require voting.

To build consensus

- Summarize the meeting or the team's work.

- Clarify any disagreements on points of view.

- Use tools to focus on and fully discuss each item.

When you feel consensus has been achieved ask, "Do we have consensus on this?"

Some groups use more formal approaches to determine whether or not they have reached consensus:

- Ask "How close are we to consensus?" People show hands to indicate their feelings. Five fingers means "I'm on board," four fingers is "I'm close," one finger indicates "we have a long way to go," a closed fist states "we aren't even close."

- Ask "Is anybody standing outside of consensus?" An affirmative answer to this questions means "I'll go along with this but I'm not really happy with it." This response may be accompanied by an explanation. Resolution may move forward.

- Ask "Is anybody blocking consensus?" An affirmative answer to this question indicates that the decision may not move forward until resolution is accomplished.

The act of building consensus is in itself a learning exercise. Participants must actively consider the reasons for their beliefs.

Establishing and Maintaining Ground Rules

Stage for learner: 1, 2, 3, or 4

Context for learning: Semiformal

Learning styles best accommodated: Activist, Pragmatist, Reflector

Outcome of learning: Knowledge, Skill Development

Learning resources role: Provide brief directions for establishing ground rules, facilitate development of agreed-on rules.

Ground rules are statements of procedure that apply to a meeting or team or the workplace in general. Examples of ground rules include

- *Attendance:* All participants must attend each meeting. In the event of an emergency, a person who cannot attend must notify at least one participant. Those who were absent are responsible for contacting another participant to bring themselves up-to-date on the missed meeting or team activity.

- *Timeliness:* All meetings will begin and end on time. All participants will be present at the beginning of the meeting.

- *Participation:* All participants agree to express their opinions during the meeting. Griping about a decision after the meeting is not acceptable.

- *Name-calling:* This will not be tolerated. People will treat one another with respect.

These are only suggestions; they may not be the ones that will work best for your meeting. Establishing your own ground rules is part of the learning process.

Brainstorming—Generating Creative Ideas

Stage for learner: 1, 2, 3, or 4

Context for learning: Semiformal

Learning styles best accommodated: Activist, Pragmatist

Outcome of learning: Knowledge

Learning resources role: Provide brief directions for establishing ground rules, lead initial efforts.

Brainstorming is a process for generating ideas. There are minimal rules for conducting a brainstorming session. They are

- Everyone can participate. Assure participants that they should express every idea, if even it seems silly.

- It is okay to build on other people's ideas.

- Record all ideas on a flip chart.

- There is no discussion during brainstorming. Criticism or judgment is withheld until all ideas are on the board.

- Set a time limit for the brainstorming session. Fifteen minutes is usually good. You may want to start by having members write down their ideas before the discussion.

- Continue brainstorming for the entire time allotted even if there is a lull. Creative ideas sometimes surface during quiet time.

The round robin is a variation of brainstorming. Begin by identifying the issue and ask the participants to write down all of their ideas. After allowing a few minutes for thinking and recording, ask each person to offer an idea for the brainstorm list. When a participant runs out of ideas, the turn goes to the next person. The rounds continue until there are no more ideas.

Knowledge Networks—Sharing Tacit Knowledge in a Database

Stage for learner: 3 or 4

Context for learning: Nonformal

Learning styles best accommodated: Theorist, Reflector

Outcome of learning: Knowledge

Learning resources role: Obtain a network system, assist learners in understanding its use.

People at Buckman Laboratories believe that the most influential employees are those who do the most to share their knowledge with colleagues (Pan and Scarborough, 1998). The K'Netix© knowledge network facilitates sharing and serves as an organizational memory in which to store knowledge. It is designed to handle the kind of tacit, individual knowledge that is difficult to objectify and is sometimes based on personal beliefs.

The K'Netix© knowledge network is divided into two categories: organizational forums, which focus on current knowledge being generated, and a codified database, which stores new knowledge for future use. There are seven forums for online conversation: three are customer focused and four are regionally focused. Someone might post a question from a customer on the organizational forums, where it could be seen and answered by anyone in the company. If it is not answered, a forum specialist picks up the issue, identifies a specialist to investigate it, and asks if he or she would be willing to search for the answer.

The codified information is categorized as customer knowledge, competitive intelligence, process knowledge, and product knowledge. The knowledge transfer department supports the system and is responsible for reformatting forum data for the historical database. Every employee has access to the system. Before the implementation of the K'Netix© knowledge network, 16% of Buckman employees had direct relationships with their customers. By 1998, this was up to 50%, and it is expected to rise to 80%.

Whiteboards—Capturing Ideas Generated in the Cafeteria

Stage for learner: 3 or 4

Context for learning: Nonformal

Learning styles best accommodated: Theorist, Reflector

Outcome of learning: Knowledge

Learning resources role: Procure a whiteboard, publicize its use.

A simple way to capture new ideas is to place a whiteboard in the cafeteria so that people can keep track of ideas that occur to them during their coffee or lunch breaks. The ideas can be developed further at a later time or by another group of people.

11

Learning Opportunities for Leaders

> The job of a coach is to trust the students more than they trust themselves.
>
> **TIM GALLWAY**

It is critical that supervisors and managers in your organization support the learning effort. They can, without realizing it, put a damper on learning through off-hand comments like "You can't go to the learning session because we have to get the product out." Although this statement may be true, the employee might assume from this that the manager does not support learning at all. The leader needs to learn how to augment the learning process even while focusing on reaching organizational goals. For instance, if an employee wants to attend a learning session during a peak production time, the manager might ask a series of questions to help the learner reflect on the situation.

Learning Tools

Most managers need assistance in attaining skills and techniques to support learning. There are few formal classes on such skills. It may be beneficial to develop some in-house.

Facilitation Skills Workshop with Peer Coach Follow-Up

Stage for learner: 3 or 4

Context for learning: Semiformal

Learning styles best accommodated: Activist, Pragmatist, Reflector

Outcome of learning: Knowledge, Skill Development

Learning resources role: Create, publicize, and facilitate program or obtain a facilitator.

Facilitation is a critical skill in many of today's working environments. While there are many ways to learn facilitation, a workshop may be a way to begin. Adults often learn best by doing, so you may want to design the workshop to allow participants to learn facilitation skills while conducting a meeting.

Suggested topics for a facilitation skills workshop include agenda setting, establishment of purpose, establishment of ground rules, facilitator's responsibilities, participants' responsibilities, tools for generating discussion (such as brainstorming and the affinity process), and tools for coming to decisions (such as nominal group technique, multi-voting, and consensus building). As each item is presented, stop to discuss its appropriate use in a real meeting.

Provide for peer coach follow-up; when one participant facilitates a meeting, have the other attend. At the conclusion of the session, the two could debrief each other on what they learned about the facilitation process.

Coaching Skills Workshop

Stage for learner: 3 or 4

Context for learning: Semiformal

Learning styles best accommodated: Activist, Pragmatist, Reflector

Outcome of learning: Knowledge, Skill Development

Learning resources role: Create, publicize, and facilitate program or obtain a facilitator.

Create a workshop for practicing coaching skills. Begin by making sure the participants understand themselves; a thorough knowledge of self results in better coaching. If participants do not know themselves well, you may want to begin with some of the tools discussed in Chapter 6.

Use brainstorming to help participants develop an understanding of how they facilitate learning for those who report to them. Divide the group into triads to practice coaching skills. Each member of the triad has a role to play: *A* is the coach, who assists the learner in resolving a learning issue. The challenge is not to tell learners the answer but to help them think through options and make their own decisions. *B* is the learner, who brings a matter of concern to the coach, such as something he or she wants to learn, or a problem with a coworker. *C* is the observer. At the conclusion of the dialogue between the coach and the learner, the observer leads a discussion on what was learned in the process. The participants switch roles so that they all have the opportunity to play each role once.

The following are some key elements in facilitating the learning of others:

- Ask open-ended questions whenever possible.

- Do not offer a solution too soon, and when a suggestion must be made, do it in the form of a leading question, such as "Well, do you think _____ might be a good starting place?"

- Help learners learn to ask good questions.

- Encourage learners to practice different types of learning.

- Gradually increase learners' independence in making their own learning decisions.

When this workshop is completed, provide a mechanism for supporting use of the new skills, such as a learning network (see Chapter 9), which is geared toward people leading others in learning, or a coaches' clinic. This will reinforce new skills: A one-time learning event, like a workshop, does not ensure that new skills have been fully learned and internalized.

Coaches' Clinic—Learning Opportunities with Production Deadlines

Stage for learner: 2, 3, or 4

Context for learning: Nonformal

Learning styles best accommodated: Theorist, Reflector

Outcome of learning: Knowledge

Learning resources role: Publicize the clinic; facilitate or provide for facilitation of sessions.

Frontline supervisors and managers are often caught between opposing organizational forces. In what I call the "squashed tomato" approach to management, these critical organizational members are asked to live up to the mission of creating learning opportunities but are also asked to ensure timely, high-quality production or services. A coaches' clinic is not a solution, but it does at least keep management informed of the content of learning opportunities being offered. The clinic could also allow learning coaches to express some of the difficulties they have experienced with learning and to engage in a dialogue with peers that might generate ideas for resolving the issues. Offer the clinic on a monthly basis.

The coaches' clinic could be held with a small group or as part of a management meeting. If your organization has a learning center, consider holding a coaches' open house during a lunch hour. Offer sandwiches and soft drinks. Post flip charts around the room describing the various learning opportunities and their schedules. Be available to answer questions about how this program can assist coaches in getting their work done.

Summary

The learning tools described in Chapters 6 through 11 were designed to help you create a learning system by identifying the various learning opportunities with their concomitant learning stages, contexts, styles, and outcomes.

By now, you have probably selected learning tools from each chapter that will best meet your organization's needs. You may want to combine them with existing learning opportunities in a chart of your customized learning system, using Exercise 6 as a guide.

Combining your selections from Exercise 6 with those you already have in place in your organization will provide the foundation for your learning system. Over time you will refine some of the learning opportunities, drop some that are no longer valuable, and add some new ones that you create or learn about from others.

This dynamic system will assist in the development of employees who love to learn. When they are learning, your organization will become more flexible and able to respond to changes in the marketplace and your employees will be more engaged in their work—which should lead to higher levels of satisfaction for all involved.

EXERCISE 6: LEARNING OPPORTUNITY SELECTION GRID

Offering	Type of Learning			Stage of Learner				Context					Learning Style Accommodated				Outcome of Learning			
	Individual	Peer	Group	1	2	3	4	F	S	N	I		A	P	T	R	Knowledge	Attitude/Values	Skill	Aspiration

F = Formal, S = Semiformal, N = Nonformal, I = Informal, A = Activist, P = Pragmatist, T = Theorist, R = Reflector

References

Adair, J. (1999, May 5). *The Revolution from Management to Business Leadership*. Paper presented at the International Conference on Organization Development, Manama, Bahrain.

Anonymous. (1997, March 29). Education and the wealth of nations. *Economist, 34,* 17–18.

Argyris, C. (1993). Teaching smart people how to learn. In R. Howard (Ed.), *The Learning Imperative: Managing People for Continuous Innovation.* Boston: Harvard Business School Press.

Argyris, C., and Schön, D. A. (1974). *Theory in Practice: Increasing Professional Effectiveness.* San Francisco: Jossey-Bass.

Bandura, A. (Ed.). (1976). *Modeling Theory.* (2nd ed.). Chicago: Rand McNally.

Bennis, W. G., and Schein, E. H. (Eds.). (1966). *Leadership and Motivation: Essays of Douglas McGregor.* Cambridge, MA: MIT Press.

Bolles, R. N. (1999). *What Color Is Your Parachute?* Berkeley, CA: Ten-Speed Press.

Brand, A. (1998). Knowledge management and innovation at 3M. *Journal of Knowledge Management, 2*(1, September), 17–22.

Brookfield, S. D. (1991). *Developing Critical Thinkers: Challenging Adults to Explore Alternative Ways of Thinking.* San Francisco: Jossey-Bass.

Burgoyne, J., Cunningham, I., Garratt, B., Honey, P., Mayo, A., Mumford, A., Pearn, M., and Pedler, M. (1998). *A Declaration on Learning.* Maidenhead, Berkshire, UK: Learning Declaration Group.

Candy, P. C. (1991). *Self-Direction for Lifelong Learning.* San Francisco: Jossey-Bass.

Castleberg, M. (1999). *Reflective Note-Taking: A New Tool for Capturing Learning*. Milwaukee, WI: Author.

Cleese, J. (1988, May 16). No more mistakes and you're through! *Forbes*, 126–127.

Collins, J. (1999). The learning person. *Training*, 36(3, March), 84.

Cramb, J., and Cunningham, I. (1998). Face value—The case of KPMG. *People Management*, 4(16, August 13), 48–52.

Crisp Publications, Menlo Park, CA.

Cunningham, I. (1999). *The Wisdom of Strategic Learning: The Self-Managed Learning Solution*. (2nd ed.). Brookfield, VT: Gower.

Cunningham, I., Bennett, B., and Dawes, G. (Eds.). (2000). *Self-Managed Learning in Action*. London: Gower Press.

Davenport, T. O. (1999). *Human Capital: What It Is and Why People Invest It*. San Francisco: Jossey-Bass.

DeBiasio, A., MacAskill, R., Power, J., and Van der Touw, M. (1999, May 16–18). *Cominco's Learning Center: A Unique, Successful Partnership*. Paper presented at the Workplace Learning: Progress Through Innovation conference, Milwaukee, WI.

Dewey, J. (1938). *Experience and Education*. New York: Collier Books.

Dixon, N. (1994). *The Organizational Learning Cycle*. New York: McGraw-Hill.

Emery, F. E., and Emery, M. (1976). *A Choice of Futures*. Leiden, Netherlands: Maritimes Nijhoff Social Sciences Division.

Excel. (1999). *Learning Type Measure*. Barrington, IL: Excel.

Fisher, D., Merron, K., and Torbert, W. R. (1987). Human development and managerial effectiveness. *Group and Organization Studies, 12*, 257–273.

Flynn, G. (1996). *Personnel Journal*, 75(6, June), 100–108.

(1999). PG&E's learning center provides facilitation, inspiration—and recreation. http://www.workforceonline.com/members/research/teams.

Galagan, P. (1994). Reinventing the profession. *Training and Development, 48*(12, December), 20–27.

Galagan, P. A., Barron, T., and Salopek, J. (1999). Training's new guard. *Training and Development, 53*(5, May), 27–53.

Godfrey, S. (1998). Are you creative? *Journal of Knowledge Management, 2*(1, September), 14–16.

Goldberg, M. (1999). *A Perspective on Lifelong Learning*. New York: Association of Joint Labor/Management Education Programs.

Gordon, E. E., Morgan, R. R., and Ponticell, J. A. (1995). The individualized training alternative. *Training & Development* (September), 52–60.

Grolnic, S. (1999, May 16–18). *Creating Intentional Learning Environments*. Paper presented at Workplace Learning: Progress Through Innovation conference, Milwaukee, WI.

Handy, C. (1989). *The Age of Unreason*. Cambridge, MA: Harvard Business School Press.

Harlaquinn, G., Marshalek, A., Meyer, J., and Rettler, B. (1999, May 16–18). *The Evolution of Workshops at Gehl Company: When Employees and Peer Advisors Become Teachers.* Paper presented at Workplace Learning: Progress Through Innovation conference, Milwaukee, WI.

Harvey, J. B. *Learning Not to Teach.* Washington, DC: George Washington University.

Hersey, P., and Blanchard, K. H. (1988). *Management of Organizational Behavior.* (5th ed.). Englewood Cliffs, NJ: Prentice Hall.

Herzberg, F. (1968). One more time: How do you motivate employees? *Harvard Business Review, 46*(1), 53–62.

Holt, J. (1991). *How Children Learn.* London: Penguin Books.

Honey, P., and Mumford, A. (1986). *The Manual of Learning Styles.* Maidenhead, Berkshire, UK: McGraw-Hill.

Honey, P., and Mumford, A. (1992). Learning styles questionnaire facilitator guide. In P. Honey (Ed.), *Organization Design and Development.* (3rd ed.). Maidenhead, Berkshire, UK: McGraw-Hill.

Honold, L. K. (1999). *An Empowered Organization: A Consideration of Professional and Theoretical Alternatives.* Unpublished doctoral dissertation, Fielding Institute, Santa Barbara, CA.

Houle, C. O. (1961). *The Inquiring Mind.* Madison, WI: University of Wisconsin Press.

Hudson, L. (1986). *Contrary Imaginations.* London: Methuen.

Kline, P., and Saunders, B. (1993). *Ten Steps to a Learning Organization.* Arlington, VA: Great Oceans Publishers.

Knowledge PDP. (1999). http://www.knowledgeassociates.com.

Knowles, M. S. (1980). *The Modern Practice of Adult Education: From Pedagogy to Andragogy.* (Rev. ed.) Chicago: Follett.

Kolb, D. A. (1984). *Experiential Learning: Experience as the Source of Learning and Development.* Englewood Cliffs, NJ: Prentice Hall.

Kolb, D. A. (1985). *Learning Style Inventory.* Boston: McBer & Company Training Resources Group.

Kroeger, O., and Thuesen, J. M. (1988). *Type Talk: The 16 Personality Types That Determine How We Live, Love, and Work.* New York: Delta.

Kuhn, T. (1962). *The Structure of Scientific Revolution.* Chicago: University of Chicago Press.

Lankard, B. A. (1995). New ways of learning in the workplace. http://www.ed.gov/database/ERIC: ERIC.

Lindenberger, J. G., and Zachary, L. J. (1999). Play "20 questions" to develop a successful mentoring program. *Training and Development, 53*(2, February), 12–14.

Lynch, L. M., and Black, S. E. (1996). *Beyond the Incidence of Training: Evidence from a National Employer Survey.* (www.irhe.upenn.edu/eqw): University of Pennsylvania, Center on the Educational Quality of the Workforce.

Manly, D., Brost, A., and Houtman, J. (1997). *Wisconsin Workplace Partnership Training Program.* Madison, WI: Center on Education and Work, University of Wisconsin–Madison.

Marquardt, M. J. (1999). *Action Learning in Action: Transforming Problems and People for World-Class Organizational Learning.* Palo Alto, CA: Davies-Black.

Maslow, A. H. (1943). A theory of human motivation. *Psychological Review, 50*(July), 370–396.

Maslow, A. H. (1965). Some basic propositions of a growth and self-actualization psychology. In G. Lindzey and C. Hall (Eds.), *Theories of Personality: Primary Sources and Research.* New York: Van Nostrand.

Maslow, A. H. (1970). *Motivation and Personality.* (2nd ed.). New York: HarperCollins.

McAll, M. W., Lombardo, M. M., and Srooisson, A. (1988). *The Lessons of Experience.* Lexington, MA: Lexington Books.

McCain, M. L., and Pantazis, C. (1997). *Responding to Workplace Change: A National Vision for a System for Continuous Learning.* Alexandria, VA: American Society for Training and Development.

McGregor, D. (1960). *The Human Side of Enterprise.* New York: McGraw-Hill.

Mercer, M. W. (1989). *Turning Your HR Department into a Profit Center.* New York: AMACOM.

Mercer, M. W. (1993). *Hire the Best and Avoid the Rest.* New York: AMACOM.

Merriam, S. B., and Caffarella, R. S. (1999). *Learning in Adulthood: A Comprehensive Guide.* (2nd ed.). San Francisco: Jossey-Bass.

Millner, N., Walker, R., Johnson, P., Hendrix, C., McCall, S., and Stacey, G. (1999, May 16–18). *A Strategic Plan for Workplace Education for the 21st Century.* Paper presented at Workplace Learning: Progress Through Innovation conference, Milwaukee, WI.

National Center on the Educational Quality of the Workforce. (1995). *The Other Shoe: Education's Contribution to the Productivity of Establishments.* Washington, DC: Department of the Census.

Nonaka, I., and Takeuchi, H. (1995). *The Knowledge-Creating Company: How Japanese Companies Create the Dynamics of Innovation.* New York: Oxford University Press.

Ornstein, R. E. (1977). *The Psychology of Consciousness.* (2nd ed.). New York: Harcourt, Brace, Jovanovich.

Owen, H. (1997). *Open Space Technology: A User's Guide.* San Francisco: Berrett-Koehler.

Pan, S. L., and Scarborough, H. (1998). A sociotechnical view of knowledge sharing at Buckman Laboratories. *Journal of Knowledge Management, 2*(1), 55-66.

Pearce, W. B., and Littlejohn, S. (1997). *Moral Conflict: When Social Worlds Collide.* Thousand Oaks, CA: Sage.

Pedler, M., Burgoyne, J., and Boydell, T. (1991). *The Learning Company: A Strategy for Sustainable Development.* London: McGraw-Hill.

Pennings, D. (1998). Personal interview.

Peters, T. (1987). *Thriving on Chaos: Handbook for a Management Revolution.* New York: Knopf.

(1988). *The Leadership Alliance.* Des Plaines, IL: Video Publishing House.

Pfeffer, J., and Veiga, J. F. (1999). *Academy of Management Executive, 13*(2), 37–48.

Piaget, J. (1966). *Psychology of Intelligence.* Totowa, NJ: Littlefield-Adams.

Rice, C., Bell, S. F., and West, G. W. (1999, May 16–18). *Shaping Tomorrow's High Performance Workplace: An Innovative Labor/Management Partnership for Public Sector Employees.* Paper presented at the Workplace Learning: Progress Through Innovation conference, Milwaukee, WI.

Rogers, C. R. (1961). Personal thoughts on teaching and learning.

Rogers, C. R. (1983). *Freedom to Learn for the '80s.* Columbus, OH: Merrill.

Schein, E. H. (1978). *Career Dynamics: Matching Individual and Organizational Needs.* Reading, MA: Addison-Wesley.

Schön, D. A. (1983). *The Reflective Practitioner: How Professionals Think in Action.* New York: Basic Books.

Senge, P. M. (1990). *The Fifth Discipline: The Art and Practice of the Learning Organization.* New York: Doubleday.

Senge, P. M., Kleiner, A., Roberts, C., Ross, R. B., and Smith, B. J. (1994). *The Fifth Discipline Fieldbook: Strategies and Tools for Building a Learning Organization.* New York: Currency Books.

Simpson, J. A., and Weiner, F. S. C. (Eds.). (1991). *The Compact Oxford English Dictionary.* (2nd ed.). Oxford, England: Clarendon Press.

Skinner, B. F. (1974). *About Behaviorism.* New York: Knopf.

Solomon, C. M. (1994). HR facilitates the learning organization concept. *Personnel Journal, 73*(11, November), 56–66.

Spreitzer, G. M., and Quinn, R. E. (1996). Empowering middle managers to be transformational leaders. *Journal of Applied Behavioral Science, 32,* 237–261.

Stack, J. (1992). *Great Game of Business: The Only Sensible Way to Run a Company.* New York: Doubleday.

Stack, J. (1998). Great Game of Business workshop.

Stayer, R. C. (1998). Personal interview.

Stewart, D., and Ball, C. (1995). *Lifelong Learning, Developing Human Potential: An Action Agenda for Lifelong Learning for the 21st Century.* Brussels, Belgium.

Stewart, T. A. (1995). How a little company won big by betting on brainpower. *Fortune, 132*(5, September 4), 121–122.

Sunoo, B. P. (1999). Labor-management partnerships boost training. http://www.workforceonline.com/cgi: Workforce Online.

Taco, Inc. (1999). Education with a touch of TLC. http://www.taco-hvac.com.

Tannen, D. (1998). *The Argument Culture: Stopping America's War of Words.* New York: Ballantine Books.

Tetrault, A., Schriesheim, C. A., and Neider, L. L. (1989). Leadership training interventions: A review. *Organization Development Journal, 6,* 77–83.

U.S. Department of Commerce, U.S. Department of Education, U.S. Department of Labor, National Institute for Literacy, Small Business Administration. (1999). *21st Century Skills for 21st Century Jobs.* Washington, DC: U.S. Government Printing Office.

U.S. Department of Labor. (1996). *Workforce Statistics.* Washington, DC: U.S. Department of Labor.

Vaill, P. B. (1989). *Managing as a Performing Art.* San Francisco: Jossey-Bass.

Vaill, P. B. (1998). *Learning as a Way of Being.* San Francisco: Jossey-Bass.

Van de Kamp Nohl, Mary. (2000). The good screw-up. *Milwaukee Magazine,* 17.

Wallace, R. (1999). Sharing what you know—Peer mentoring at Microsoft. *At Work* (May–June), 17–19.

Watkins, K. E., and Marsick, V. J. (1993). *Sculpting the Learning Organization: Lessons in the Art and Science of Systemic Change.* San Francisco: Jossey-Bass.

Watkins, K. E., and Marsick, V. J. (1996). *In Action: Creating the Learning Organization.* Alexandria, VA: American Society for Training and Development.

Weisbord, M. R., and Janoff, S. (1995). *Future Search: An Action Guide to Finding Common Ground in Organizations and Communities.* San Francisco: Berrett-Koehler.

Wood, R., and Gilbert, L. (1996). Continuous cross-functional learning. In K. E. Watkins and V. J. Marsick (Eds.), *Creating the Learning Organization.* Alexandria, VA: American Society for Training and Development.

Wycoff, J., and Snead, L. (1999). Stimulating innovation with collaboration rooms. *Journal for Quality and Participation, 22*(2, March/April), 55–57.

Yankelovich, D. (1999). *The Magic of Dialogue: Transforming Conflict into Cooperation.* New York: Simon & Schuster.

Zubroff, S. (1998). *In the Age of the Smart Machine: The Future of Work and Power.* New York: Basic Books.

Index